ORDER FORM

To: Consolidated Press International
3171-A South 129th East Ave., Ste 338
Tulsa, OK 74134

Please ship to me at the address shown below the following number of copies of books at $11.95 each. Enclosed is my check or money order for $_____ which includes $2.50 (each)[1] for shipping and handling. (Oklahoma residents add .65 @ book state sales tax).

Kill Zone; A Sniper Looks at Dealey Plaza $_____

JFK; The Dead Witnesses   _____

     Shipping and Handling @ $2.50 ea.   _____

     Oklahoma Sales Tax (OK only)   _____

     TOTAL AMOUNT ENCLOSED   _____

Ship to:
Name_____

Address_____

City _____

State _____ Zip _____

---

[1] Bulk orders will be shipped at standard rates as specified by customer.

Kill Zone

A Sniper Looks At Dealey Plaza

An Original Publication of *Typhoon Press*

A Division of Christian Patriot Press

ISBN: 0-9639062-0-8

First Typhoon Press printing: January 1994

10 9 8 7 6 5 4 3 2

Typhoon Press is a trademark of Christian Patriot Press, an imprint of Consolidated Press International (CPI), 3171-A South 129th East Ave, Suite 338, Tulsa, OK 74134.

Printed in U.S.A.

Books by Craig Roberts

Police Sniper (Pocket Books, 1993)

Combat Medic—Vietnam (Pocket Books, 1991)

Books by Craig Roberts and Charles W. Sasser

One Shot—One Kill; America's Combat Snipers (Pocket Books, 1990)

The Walking Dead; A Marine's Story of Vietnam (Pocket Books, 1989)

ACKNOWLEDGEMENTS

Of the scores of people who assisted the author in the seven-year investigation that led to this book, I would especially like to thank:

Allen Appel, an outstanding author in his own right, for serving as editor-in-chief and devil's advocate;

My father, William F. Roberts, Jr., Senior Editor of Strebor Publications, for editorial assistance and for keeping me on track and motivated; Charles W. Sasser and Ed Wheeler for their editorial assistance and constant encouragement; researchers J. Gary Shaw and Larry Harris (co-authors of *Cover-up*), John Armstrong, Mike Farrell, Tom Keith, and Jack White (editor and producer of *The Many Faces of Lee Harvey Oswald*), for their invaluable assistance in research and for sharing information from their own investigations—and to Ed Hoffman, the most dangerous (to the government) witness at Dealey Plaza that fateful day, who assisted with the facts.

I would also like to thank those individuals in the Securities Exchange Commission, the Pentagon, the Library of Congress, the National Archives, and other various governmental entities that for obvious reasons must remain unnamed who provided information that overcame many strategically placed roadblocks.

And I would especially like to thank Jim Marrs, author of *Crossfire—The Plot That Killed Kennedy* for tieing up the loose ends—and providing the final clue: The Red Seal Note.

We thought we ranked above the chance of ill.
Others might fall, not we, for we were wise—
Merchants in freedom. So, of our free-will
We let our servants drug our strength with lies.
The pleasure and the poison had its way
On us as on the meanest, till we learned
That he who lies will steal, who steals will slay.
Neither God's judgment nor man's heart was turned.

Rudyard Kipling
The Covenant
1914

"I wonder what the King is up to tonight."

Camelot

Contents

KILL ZONE

Introduction

It was a sunny day in Dallas, unusually warm for the Fall. It had rained briefly that morning, but after the small squall line had moved through, the gray sky quickly began breaking up into small puffy white cumulus clouds. By noon, it was quite clear and beginning to grow hot.

It was the fall of 1986, and I was taking an afternoon off from a law enforcement convention that I had been attending in Dallas. Even though the heat would raise the humidity to an uncomfortable level, it would still be a good day to get away from the hotel and see a few sights. Not having any particular interest in the activities scheduled that afternoon, I decided to make use of my rental car to see what local historical landmarks might be visited prior in the hours remaining before the evening banquet.

I scanned the city map provided by the hotel desk and quickly noted the name "Dealey Plaza." Though I was not a student of the Kennedy assassination, I felt that visiting an historic site as a tourist to simply say I've been there, was enough reason to make the drive. And besides, was this also not the scene of the Murder of the Century? For a career police officer, it would be almost unforgivable to at least not take a look at the scene of the crime.

Little did I realize that this innocent sightseeing jaunt would thrust me into an investigation that would last seven years, take me into the

INTRODUCTION

shadowy world of clandestine operations that few people even realize exists, expose some of the darkest secrets of behind-the-scenes international power brokers, and bring to light a "government" that has, for the past five decades, operated above the law—under the pretext of national security.

In the pages of this book the reader will be presented evidence of a secret government, an organization that lies both within the halls of congress, the offices of the Pentagon and the White House, and certain, very special, individuals outside of—and often above—those institutions.

Kill Zone will present the missing pieces to a decades-old puzzle that will explain why, and how, certain mysterious things in history have happened. Things that were presented to the American people in a cleaned-up history book version suitable for public consumption. Only now, the veil of deceit is finally removed. Now, the sinister entity that Winston Churchill referred to as the "High Cabal," and Col. Fletcher Prouty dubbed the "Power Elite," is exposed for what it actually is. And more importantly, *who* it is.

Finally, after decades of deception, the crimes, conspiracies and coverups of The Entity—the powers behind the throne—are brought into the light. And when the pieces of the puzzle are assembled, the picture becomes a revelation.

Part I

The Kill Zone

...What thou seest, write in a book...

Revelation 1:11

"I believe in all of my heart that the shots came from behind the picket fence."

Beverly Oliver
Witness to the shooting

"...I focused in on a gentleman with a suit and a hat here at the picket fence. I saw a puff of smoke, and a man with a rifle...I was shocked..."

Ed Hoffman
Witness on the Triple
Underpass

"Lee Harvey Oswald was the assassin...the Commission found no evidence of a conspiracy, either foreign or domestic."

Gerald Ford
Member of the
Warren Commission

Chapter 1

Ambush in Dallas

After arriving at Dealey Plaza, I parked the car and walked up the steps of the Texas School Book Depository building, casually glancing back over my shoulder at the open grassy area of the Plaza as I neared the front door. There was nothing remarkable about the grassy area; it was simply an open triangular-shaped park that was bordered by east-west streets the north and south sides. At the east end a pair of white masonry monuments straddled a third east-west street that bisected the park, and at the west was a concrete overpass that arched over the three streets that funneled together at that point. I knew from some of the news reels I had seen in the past that the infamous Grassy Knoll and the monument retaining wall on which Abraham Zapruder stood to take his famous film were on the north side, just beyond some trees that blocked my vision. I entered the building.

The 5th, 6th, and 7th floors were no longer used as a warehouse. It had become a commercialized tourist attraction that weakly impersonated a museum. The main floor was a gift shop where tickets were sold to those who wished to ascend to the 6th floor. And for some unexplained reason, cameras were forbidden.

I surrendered my camera, paid my money and entered the elevator. A few minutes later I knew that my government had taken great pains to lie to the American people for the previous twenty-three years.

In 1963, the 6th floor was an open warehouse-type storage loft stacked with rows of brown cardboard boxes filled with books. Now it was a large, fairly open room interspersed with various displays, diagrams and enlarged photographs that focused on that tragic event that had occurred so many years before. I studied the diagrams and photos and read the descriptions with mild interest. I already knew the story; Lee Harvey Oswald, a known communist with mental problems, had shot President John F. Kennedy. He was later apprehended by the Dallas police, but before he could go to trial, he was shot by Jack Ruby. Every American school kid knew this version of the events of that day. We had been taught it as part of our history classes, and even the encyclopedias recorded the Oswald/lone gunman scenario as gospel truth.

As I wandered around the exhibits, I thought back to the day that altered history. It was the 22nd of November, 1963. I was a senior in high school, sitting in drafting class waiting for the teacher to call roll after returning from lunch. All of a sudden the PA system crackled with an announcement: President Kennedy had been shot in Dallas, and he had just been rushed to a hospital. We looked at each other, wondering who had sneaked into the school office during lunch and gained access to the public address system. Surely it was some type of practical joke.

But then the announcement was followed by radio news reporters describing the events that were unfolding in Dallas in excited voices. It was no joke.

I leaned over to my best friend and whispered, "Well, they finally got him."

"Yeah, too bad it wasn't before the invasion."

Those were common sentiments throughout the south and midwest, neither my friend or I had any love for JFK. He was the guy who had called off the air support for the Bay of Pigs invasion, dooming it to failure, then almost plunged us into a nuclear war with Russia over the Cuban Missile Crisis. Now, he was actively talking about getting us out

4

of Vietnam, which meant that another of Eisenhower's dominos would fall to communism. This man, our president, was gutless. And for a conservative generation that had been born at the end of World War II, to parents who had fought valiantly in that war, and who had grown up on a steady diet of patriotic war movies and documentaries, we could not imagine an America that would bow down to anyone—especially those evil Reds that we had learned about *every year* in Social Studies. Because of our apprehension of having an east coast liberal in the White House, many of us had actively campaigned for Nixon, and were shocked when Kennedy and Johnson "won" the election by a mere 100,000 votes. Even though LBJ sent me to Vietnam eighteen months later as part of the first Marine Battalion Landing Team to see combat in that Asian country, I felt that fate had dictated a favorable turn of events for American international policy when Oswald shot Kennedy. Unlike the media's portrayal of national shock and grief over Kennedy's death, many people actually felt relieved.

But this hot day in Dallas would alter that for me. Not because of any change in personal politics or loyalties, but of another, entirely different factor: a gut-wrenching, instantaneous realization that I, along with every other patriotic American, had been duped.

After wandering around the floor for a few minutes, I turned my attention to the window in the southeast corner—the infamous Sniper's Nest. The actual window where Oswald had supposedly fired the shots had been enclosed within a small glass partition which made it inaccessible to direct scrutiny. But the window to its right was outside the glass wall. I walked up to it and looked down.

I immediately felt like I had been hit with a sledge hammer. The word that came to mind at what I saw as I looked down through the window to Elm Street and the kill zone was: *Impossible!*

I knew instantly that Oswald could not have done it. At least not alone. Oswald could not have possibly fired three shots in rapid succession—5.6 seconds according to the museum displays—with a worn-out military surplus Mannlicher-Carcano mounted with a cheap telescopic sight from *that* particular location to the kill zone I now examined in more detail on the street below. The reason I *knew* that Oswald could not have done it, was because *I* could not have done it.

KILL ZONE

Unlike Oswald, who failed to qualify on the rifle range in Boot Camp, and who barely qualified "Marksman"—the lowest of three grades—on a later try, I was a trained and combat-experienced Marine sniper. I had spent a year in Vietnam, during which time I had numerous occasions to line up living, breathing human beings in the crosshairs of my precision Unertl scope and squeeze the trigger of my bolt-action Model 70 Winchester and send a .30 caliber match-grade round zipping down range.

Here I was, a professional police officer and writer, looking down at the most famous ambush site in history through the eyes of a sniper. A strange feeling came over me. A feeling of calm, dampening my anger. The trained investigator inside me surfaced and took over my emotions. I began to scrutinize what my senses were absorbing.

First, I analyzed the scene as a sniper. In the time allotted, and in the distance along the street in which the rounds had impacted the target from first report to final shot, it would take a minimum of two people shooting. There was little hope that I alone, even if armed with the precision equipment I had used in Vietnam, would be able duplicate the feat described by the Warren Commission. So if I couldn't, I reasoned, Oswald couldn't.

Unless he had help.

I looked at the engagement angle. It was entirely wrong. The wall of the building in which the windows overlooked Dealey Plaza ran east and west. By looking directly down at the *best* engagement angle—which was straight out the window facing south—I could see Houston Street. Houston was perpendicular to the wall and ran directly toward my window. This is the street on which the motorcade had approached and would have been my second choice as a zone of engagement. My first choice was directly below the window, at a drastic bend in the street that had to be negotiated by Kennedy's limousine. It would have to slow appreciably, almost to a stop, and when it did, the target would be presented moving at its slowest pace. The last zone of engagement I would pick would be as the limo drove away toward the west—and the Grassy Knoll. Here, from what I could see, three problems arose that would influence my shots. First, the target was moving away at a drastic angle to the right from the

6

window, meaning that I would have to position my body to compete with the wall and a set of vertical water pipes on the left frame of the window to get a shot. This would be extremely difficult for a right-handed shooter. Second, I would have be ready to fire exactly when the target emerged past some tree branches that obscured the kill zone. Finally, I would have to deal with two factors at the same time: the curve of the street, and the high-to-low angle formula—a law of physics Oswald would not have known.

Even if I waited for the target to pass the primary and secondary engagement zones, and for some reason decided to engage instead in the worst possible area, I still had to consider the fact that Oswald made his farthest, and most difficult shot, last. I estimated the range for this shot at between 80 and 90 yards. It was this final shot that, according to the Warren Commission, struck Kennedy's head.

As an experienced sniper, something else bothered me. Any sniper knows that the two most important things to be considered in selecting a position are the fields of fire, and a route of escape. You have to have both. It is of little value to take a shot, then not be able to successfully get away to fight another day. Even if the window was a spot that I would select for a hide, I had doubts about my ability to escape afterwards. According to what little I had read, the elevator was stuck on a floor below at the time in question, and only the stairway could have been used as a means of withdrawal. And there were dozens of people—potential witnesses—below who would be able to identify anyone rushing away from the scene. Not good.

But Oswald was not a trained or experienced military sniper. He was supposed to be little more than some odd-ball with a grudge. And for whatever reason, had decided to buy a rifle and shoot the President of the United States. Or so the Warren Commission would have us believe.

It is important at this point to demonstrate exactly what would have had to happen that warm November day in 1963 on this very floor. To do this, the reader must become Lee Harvey Oswald.

For the sake of argument, let us assume that the Warren Commission was correct in their findings. Oswald, the lone nut, was the only shooter to fire at the President. He managed to smuggle his

7

rifle up to the 6th floor, realizing well in advance that the motorcade would pass through Dealey Plaza below on his lunch hour—which is the only open kill zone on the route— and was well-prepared to take as many shots as he could at the open convertible (which he didn't even know would be uncovered that day, nor did anyone know that the motorcade would detour to Elm for a turn back to the west by the Book Depository unless they caught a late issue of the newspaper).

To see what would have had to transpire on the 22nd of November, 1963, to accomplish what the Warren Commission stated "Oswald" did, we must return to the scene of the crime and recreate the events. We must look at Dealey Plaza—through a sniper's eyes. It is only this way, with the information presented here, that one can begin to comprehend how false the Warren Commission's verdict was:

It's a warm, muggy November day. But only two windows on the 6th Floor are opened in the un-airconditioned building. You are sweating, both because of the heat and because of what you are getting ready to do. Your plans are just about to culminate in your chance to change history (for whatever motive). You look at your watch. It's almost time. You pick up your rifle and kneel at the window overlooking Elm Street. Even though there is a large crowd below, you are unconcerned about being seen—even with the weapon.

For some unfathomable reason, you have picked a confined area of Elm Street as your kill zone. You have disregarded Houston Street, which is aligned perfectly with your corner of the building, affording you a straight head-on shot for over a block where the motorcade will move slowly toward you. But shooting Kennedy from the front, where he is most vulnerable, is not what you intend to do. You have decided, for some reason to shoot Kennedy in the back, through the trees, on a winding street, at a relatively steep vertical angle, in a partially obscured, confined area that is barely visible from the window on the Elm side.

Now it's time. The motorcade is approaching. You work the bolt on the Carcano, chambering an unpredictable round-nosed 6.5mm cartridge. You bring the short-barreled carbine to your shoulder (it wasn't really a rifle), and sight through the misaligned, non-boresighted scope with defective optics and loose mount, and study the thin crosshairs. Your field of view is almost non-existent. You note that you can barely pick out one or two people in the circular lens. To bring this weapon on target after the recoil of a shot will be challenging, to say the least.

You wait. The motorcade turns the corner onto Elm, each vehicle almost stopping as they negotiate the 120 degree turn. Then you see the President. He looks different in person, alive, human. And there's Jackie. And Connally...

You are not looking though the scope now. You are simply watching the cars move slowly down Elm. You wait for a few seconds as they come into your kill zone, then raise the scope to your eye, taking a second to establish the proper eye-relief between your eyeball and the lens so that "half-moon shadows" don't appear on the edge of the sight picture. After all, the crosshairs and scope have to be exactly aligned or you will miss the target entirely. And this *has* to be done after every shot.

But wait, you are not a trained sniper. You have no idea of the "high-low" formula, or the minute-of-angle rule. You don't realize that a sniper, shooting from high to low angle, has to aim low. You don't realize that if you don't aim low at the range you have selected, that you will miss the target by up to a foot. No one has told you that because of the effects of gravity, the bullet will not drop an appreciable amount—like it did on the rifle range which was a flat-trajectory shot.

Maybe sweat is not stinging your eyes, and maybe your hands aren't shaking even though you have never killed anyone before and are now about to do so. But more than likely, you find it hard to hold the rifle on target. But you must. Seconds are ticking by and you will miss your chance. Don't worry about the time, concentrate on the crosshairs. But wait, no one ever told you to do that. Instead, you are watching the target, which is clear in your scope, and your crosshairs are a blur—exactly the opposite of what must occur for an accurate shot.

Never mind. You have other problems to contend with. Your adrenalin is pumping and you find your arms acting like they are detached from your body. Somehow you manage to regain mental control of your limbs, and at the same time attempt to control your breathing. What did they say on the rifle range in the Marines? Oh yes, "BRASS." Breath, Relax, Aim, Slack, Squeeze. That's it.

You hold your breath, try your best to relax, aim the weapon—centering on the head of the President of the United States in your scope, take up the slack from the trigger and squeeze...

The first shot jolts you back to reality. You've done it! But did you hit anything? Now your adrenalin is *really* pumping as your curiosity makes you glance quickly at the street below while you take the weapon away from your line of vision to work the bolt, chambering a fresh round.

You realign, sight in again as the dark blue Lincoln begins to disappear around the bend behind that damned tree. Screw it. Shoot. This time you manage to get the shot off a little faster. "Buck Fever" has subsided a bit. Still, you aren't sure if you hit anything because in your haste you jerked the trigger—you didn't have time for a proper squeeze. You work the bolt again, ejecting the spent casing to the right and across the room into the cardboard boxes—or at least that's where it should have gone.

Your last shot. The car is now at maximum range—actually almost out of view—but miraculously, for some reason, the car slows almost to a complete stop. You even see the brake lights come on. You shoot. Unknown to you this round hits Connally. All of a sudden the car speeds up and dashes away under the triple overpass.

Elapsed time so far since the first shot, 5.6 seconds! Not bad, considering that it takes a minimum of 3.3 seconds to fire, work the bolt, and fire again—and then only if you don't take time to accurately realign the rifle on the target before the next shot.

It's time to get away. You pull back from the window and sprint to the opposite end of the 6th floor, noting that there still is not a single person who has come up from the floor below to investigate the noise of the shots. You find a place between some boxes to hide the carbine. You didn't note, in your haste, that you left your lunch sack and a pop bottle that would undoubtedly contain your finger prints behind at the window, and nearby, only a few inches from the wall, just to the right of the window, are the three expended 6.5mm casings—neatly grouped as if they'd been placed there on purpose. Mysteriously, there *is no stripper clip which should have fallen to the floor through the magazine floor plate—and the weapon could not have functioned without it!*

You race down the stairs to the second floor (the elevator is stuck on a floor below) and enter the coffee room. You have time to fish some change out of your pocket, buy a coke, and drink half of it in the few seconds it took for a policeman to rush into the Depository, charge up one flight of stairs and charge up to the door of the room. He notes that you are standing casually by the Coke machine, haven't broken a sweat, and that you seem calm, breathing normally. This feat in itself is quite remarkable considering that you had to run completely across the 6th floor after taking your last shot, maneuvering around stacks of boxes as you raced away from your "sniper's nest," to the opposite (northwest) corner of the warehouse to the stair well. You then had to race unseen down four flights of stairs, then across the building's second floor to the coffee room where you had time to fish a dime from your pocket, buy the Coke from the vending machine, and drink half of it—all in one minute or less from the time the final shot was fired! (According the Gerald Posner in his "Oswald-did-it-the-Warren-Commission-was-right"book *Case Closed,* this is what *had* to have happened for Oswald to have accomplished his single- sniper feat).

KILL ZONE

The policeman, Dallas motorcycle officer Marrion Baker, asks your boss if you are an employee. When this is confirmed, he breaks away to search the floors above.

A few seconds later, after Baker is out of sight, you make your getaway. But instead of taking some pre-planned mode of transportation out of town, you simply walk out the front door where you run into NBC reporter Robert McNeil who asks directions to the nearest telephone. You deal with him in a very calm, collected manner, then go home to your rented room. You know that you will soon be missed at work, that the Dallas police will begin rounding up anyone in the vicinity to question almost immediately, but you still don't try to escape by leaving the city. Even if you decided at the last moment to attempt such a move, you wouldn't be able to get very far on the $17.00 you have in your pocket. Instead, you decide to take a walk—outside, in public view.

Twenty-three years after those shots were fired, I walked away from the window in disgust. I had seen all I needed to know that Oswald could not have been the lone shooter. As I walked toward the elevator I began to look at the scene as a police officer. If one could forget that the victim was the President of the United States and this was a political assassination, and simply worked the scene as a standard homicide, perhaps it could be put into manageable perspective. The next thing that would have to be done would be to examine the rest of Dealey Plaza.

A homicide scene is not simply the place the body was found. It is the entire area of influence that might contain clues. In this case, crime scene was anywhere within range of a high-powered rifle.

I walked out of the Book Depository and crossed the street. I stopped for a moment and looked around. There were several possible spots for a second shooter—which meant that more than two riflemen could have been positioned. Exactly what positions were utilized depended upon the physical trajectories of the bullets that had been fired. That would come later.

I walked all around Dealey Plaza, exploring any spot that I felt might serve the purpose of a sniper. Finally I arrived at the Grassy

12

Knoll and the Picket Fence, which I had purposely saved for last. I walked up the slope and around the fence, arriving in a parking lot that was bordered on the northwest by train tracks. I walked the length of the fence, stopping at a spot on the eastern end.

I looked over the fence at Elm Street and froze. This is exactly where I would position myself if I wanted the most accurate shot possible considering the terrain I had explored. It had some drawbacks—it was close to witnesses, and prone to pre-incident discovery—but the advantages far outweighed the disadvantages for a determined assassin. The target vehicle would be *approaching* instead of moving away, thereby continually decreasing the range; the shot would be almost flat trajectory, making the down-angle formula a mute point; the deflection (right/left angle) would change little until the car passed a freeway sign on the north curbline; and finally, it offered numerous escape route possibilities. Behind me, to the north and west, was a parking lot full of cars, a train yard full of boxcars, and several physical terrain features to use as cover during withdrawal. It was by far the best spot.

Looking almost due east, across the grassy open park-like Plaza, I could see two multi-story office-type buildings approximately the same height as the Depository. The roof tops of either building would be excellent firing positions for a trained rifleman with the proper equipment, and would be the places I would select if I wanted the best possible chance of not being detected in advance. Without going to the roofs of each, I could not determine the accessibility of escape routes. But for firing platforms, they were ideal.

Then, considering the possibility of multiple-snipers (which meant a conspiracy), I had to ask myself how I would position the shooters to cover the kill zone in front of the Grassy Knoll?

My military training once again took over. I would use an area within the Plaza that would afford the best kill zone for either a crossfire or triangulated fire. Simply put, I would position my teams in such a way that their trajectory of fire converged on the most advantageous point to assure a kill. In the military, single snipers are seldom used. Normally, the smallest sniper team consists of two men, a sniper and his spotter/security man. Even in police SWAT teams, a marksman has an observer who is equipped with a spotting scope or binoculars to help pick and identify targets and handle the radio communications.

In this case, I would position at least one team behind the Picket Fence (more if I wanted to secure the rear against intruders), another on one or both of the two office buildings (which I later found to be the Dallas County Records Building and the County Criminal Courts Building), and possibly a team on a building across the street north of the Records Building known at the time as the Dal-Tex building. I would have never put anyone in the School Book Depository with so many locations that were much more advantageous—unless I needed diversion. If I did, it would be a good place for red herrings to be observed by witnesses.

By this time it was growing late. The banquet started in an hour, and I still had to make my way through Dallas traffic back to the hotel. It had been more than an interesting day. It had been a day in which I had discovered that the United States Government had lied to me all of my adult life. The same government that had sent me to Vietnam, had sacrificed over 58,000 of my peers for no discernable gain, and had withdrawn from Southeast Asia after supposedly securing Nixon's "Peace with Honor."

Honor? I had just discovered what I later found so many others had discovered before. A *coup d' etat* had occurred, and then had successfully been covered up at the highest levels of government for over a quarter of a century. I found it hard to sleep that night.

The assassination of John F. Kennedy was not the issue. It was the fact that the government, *my* government, had lied to me. As a police officer sworn to uphold the law, there are no stratus levels in criminals. A liar, a thief, or a murderer is exactly that. There is no one who has the privilege to commit a crime without prosecution. Every rookie of every police academy in the country learns one thing above all: *no one is above the law!*

Not even the President of the United States—*or those who control him.*

Chapter 2

The Investigation Begins

When I returned home, I dug out some video tapes that I had recorded on the twentieth anniversary of the assassination. At the time, I was busily working on my book *One Shot—One Kill; America's Combat Snipers* which I was co-writing with my old police partner and former homicide detective, Charles W. Sasser. Because we were so busy, I did not take time to watch the programs when they were broadcast. I had simply fed the tapes into the VCR, hit the record button, and had gone back to work. The tapes would become research material I would add to my library for future reference should they ever be needed. I was now glad I had.

I watched each with interest. I noted that there seemed to be several schools of thought on the controversy concerning who shot JFK, each reinforced by the particular critic or researcher featured. There seemed to be five basic categories: The Mafia; the CIA; Castro; the anti-Castro Cubans; and finally the Communists. This last category had many sub-branches: Russians, Chinese, Latins, and finally, our own domestic Reds. I could see that most of the various authors, researchers and Warren Commission critics had fallen into a syndrome that often plagues the amateur detective. They had taken up a given line of thinking and had become inflexible on admitting the existence of contradictory data. This is like someone who goes down a dead-end street, then even after finding that the street does not go through, refuses to read any other street signs to find the thoroughfare. Taking this syndrome to the extreme, the person then does everything possible to defend his decision and "prove" that this is indeed the one and only thoroughfare.

This in itself creates false leads for others. Instead of putting several pieces of a puzzle together, we find ourselves with only a few of the pieces, none of which connect to form a complete picture. And to make matters worse, stubbornly sticking to a theory while extolling its virtues tends to draw more supporters. Then, instead of a thorough, unbiased investigation, one has theory candidates being voted on by the number of supporters each theory draws. Instead of an investigation that proceeds down logical avenues, we have a contest that has no winners. This is exactly what I would try to orchestrate if I wanted to cover up a crime and had the power to do so. It is not a hard thing to do. It is simply a matter of leaving false leads and bogus evidence—known to cops as "throw downs"—and maybe eliminating a few, if not all, of the witnesses. What remains is contradiction, and contradiction is the roadblock to truth.

On one of my video tapes was a very clear copy of the footage taken by Abraham Zapruder from the steps of the concrete pergola east of the Grassy Knoll. I watched intently as the motorcade approached the camera. The blue Lincoln carrying the President, Jackie, Governor Connally and his wife, and the two Secret Service Agents, Kellerman and Greer, disappeared for a few seconds behind a large metal sign, then reappeared with Kennedy clutching at this throat with both hands. I grabbed the remote control and backed the tape up, thinking immediately that when that film was taken, no one in those days would have a clue that in the future almost every American home would have the capability of running film forward, in reverse, and in slow motion at the push of a button. This could get interesting.

Again the limo disappeared behind the sign with Kennedy waving at the crowd, then emerged with him holding both arms up to clutch his throat. I let the tape run.

THE KILL ZONE

Kennedy seemed to slump slightly forward, then *bang!* His head virtually exploded in a cloud of red mist. I froze the picture, then backed it up. I ran it again, and again. There was no question about it; John F. Kennedy had been shot from the right front. That would put the shooter in exactly the spot I had selected in Dallas—behind the Picket Fence on the Grassy Knoll.

How in the world could anyone look at that film and say that the fatal head strike had come from the rear? The so-called experts who stated that the rearward jerk of Kennedy's head was due to "muscle reaction," "jet force from an erupting bullet," or some other violation of the law of physics, had obviously never served in combat where witnessing high-velocity bullet strikes was commonplace. Simply said, if one places a softball on top of a fence post, then hits it with a baseball bat, it only goes in one direction—away from the force. Even if it is securely anchored down with springs or surgical tubing to serve as "neck muscles."

Some of the supporters of the Warren Commission, according to one of the tapes, stated that the bullet came from the rear because the eruption of brain matter and blood came out of the front of the President's skull. I saw something else. In a head shot, the exit wound, due the build up of hydrostatic pressure, explodes in a conical formation in the down-range direction of the bullet. Yet in the Zapruder film, I could plainly see that the eruption was not a conical shape to the front of the limo, but instead was an explosion that cast fragments both up and down in a vertical plane, and side to side in a horizontal plane. There was only one explanation for this: an exploding, or "frangible" bullet. Such a round explodes upon impact—in exactly the manner depicted on the film.

I was familiar with such bullets. They were easy to make, and reputedly were the favored weapon of certain international assassins. While in Vietnam, the conversation among snipers often turned to ammunition and ballistics. In one particular conversation the subject of dum-dum bullets came up. Though outlawed by the Geneva Convention, such rounds were known to exist in the covert world. The most basic frangible, or disintegrating, bullet is a soft-core bullet with a "X" carved deeply across the nose. Fragments remain after such a

17

bullet is shot, but are hard to identify as far as rifling marks are concerned. Other descriptions included hollow-point bullets filled with explosive material, and hollowed out bullets filled with mercury, then sealed with paraffin. No matter how the round was constructed, it was definitely an exploding round. And it was fired from the front.

One tape featured some doctor who presented himself as an expert filled with wisdom in the world of bullet wounds. I would have loved to put this guy on the witness stand. He went into a long dissertation of how there is a cadaveric muscle reaction that forced the head back into the direction the shot came from, assisted by a "jet effect" of exploding brain tissue issuing forth from the front of the skull. I rolled my eyes and didn't know whether to laugh or cry. I knew that his "expertise" had most likely been gained by examining gunshot victims that had been wheeled into a hospital emergency room sometime after the fact, or long dead cadavers laying stiff in some morgue. Any first year intern who examines a standard bullet wound can judge direction of travel by a simple rule of thumb: an entrance wound is small and an exit wound is large. But how many doctors have ever had the opportunity to witness the shot at the moment of impact? Especially a head shot fired at long range by a high-powered rifle? Unless they served in the infantry during combat, very few indeed.

I wanted to give this particular doctor a class on national television pertaining to ballistics. The formula for the impact of an object is Force = 1/2 Mass x Velocity squared. In the case of a 6.5mm Carcano bullet, which weighs 161 grains and travels at 2100 feet per second, the force of the mass that struck President Kennedy was in excess of 50,000 pounds per square inch! Kennedy's head had no choice but to go in the direction of force. That is exactly what we saw in Vietnam, and that is what had happened on the Zapruder film.

I shut the television off and contemplated what I had just witnessed. It was the murder of the century and I was convinced that it remained unsolved. After a few minutes I knew what I had to do.

I had to investigate a homicide.

Past experiences had equipped me to stand up to anyone who tried to perpetuate the lie that there was no conspiracy and that Oswald had acted alone—case closed. I was a trained professional investigator with over 18 years experience at the time; I had been a combat experienced sniper and had qualified Expert on virtually every weapon used in an infantry battalion between 1964 and 1987 (active and reserve); I was also a master-ranked shooting team member of both the police department and the military, and I was a writer who had already written two respected books on sniping, *One Shot—One Kill*, and *Police Sniper*. These last qualifications would prove invaluable. The contacts I made during the research and writing of those books would open doors to me that no "assassination researcher" had ever gained access to or even knew existed.

And there was a fourth qualification that I could add to the list: I was a commercial pilot and aircraft mechanic with both flight and maintenance experience on a large number of light, medium and heavy aircraft. Little did I know how important this last qualification would become in the coming months.

There are certain elements that must be addressed during any investigation, especially one for murder. Basically, the elements are as follows: There has to be a crime committed; there has to be a crime scene; you must develop suspects; the suspects normally must have motives; and finally, the suspects must have both the means and the opportunity to carry out the crime.

These factors established, there must also be evidence.

According to Blackstone's much quoted *Commentaries*, "Evidence signifies that which demonstrates, makes clear, or ascertains the truth of the very fact or point in issue, either on the one side or on the other..."

Evidence falls into two categories: Direct and Real. Direct evidence is that which is provided by witness testimony. Real evidence is in the nature of such physical items as weapons, tool marks, fingerprints and so on. Witness testimony falls into various categories that range from eye witness accounts to expert testimony given by an expert witness such as a medical examiner or a qualified ballistics technician.

Besides all of the above elements, there are the basic questions that must be asked and answered by the investigator. These are, in the case of this particular conspiracy, very basic: Who did it? Who ordered it done? What was the motive? How was it done? Who covered it up? And finally, *who benefitted?*

It was time to begin the first phase of the investigation: Research. A myriad of books, articles, documentaries and video presentations have been produced in the years since the murder, but most, as mentioned, seemed to have been created to serve as reinforcement to a particular writer or researcher. Still, almost all of them contained valuable facts that, if indisputable, could provide a framework for the investigation. Each, I found, had gaps that were filled in by speculation. This was to be expected. If there were no gaps, the case would have been solved long ago. The challenge would be to take the facts, build a sequence of events, put the players in place, then try to tie everything together. It would not be necessary to cover every minute detail, for in a court of law the case is normally won by a preponderance of evidence and testimony presented by one side or the other. The final result is a decision that is made after sufficient evidence has been presented to lead a reasonable man to decide the issue. This is called finding a verdict "beyond a reasonable doubt." It does not take a confession on the part of the defendant, nor even their testimony. However, I was to find in this case that more than sufficient evidence had already surfaced and been presented that not only verified that a conspiracy had existed, but that in any other murder case would have demanded that the case to be reopened and investigated. There is no statute of limitations on murder. Competent law enforcement officers from the jurisdiction in which the crime occurred should have been directed to reopen the files and again investigate the case using the latest in technology. But this has not happened.

It is probable that it will not happen, as it would require the cooperation of the federal government. The unseen powers in Washington would have to agree to release documents and evidence to the jurisdiction, holding nothing back under the guise of National Security. The problem with this last item is that the government, since the World War II years, has made it a practice to over-classify the security levels on documents, and on far too many occasions, seal files for National Security. I was to find this to be an old saw used on almost every occasion where a critical piece of evidence was missing from the puzzle.

The research began with the viewing of the rest of the video tapes I had recorded. Most were repetitious, or hammered on a particular theory. But several valid points were made. I noted each for future investigation.

Then, as I watched one particular scene, something grabbed my attention. The scene was the famous footage of Air Force One parked on the ramp at Andrews Air Force Base. It was the night of the assassination and the airplane had just returned to Washington with the body of JFK. The action taking place was the lowering of the casket from the aft left entry door to a waiting Navy ambulance. In watching this footage, it is difficult to pay attention to anything except the gantry that is slowly lowering the casket to the ground. Besides the coffin and the somber looking men in suits that surround it, the viewer's eyes are drawn to Jacqueline Kennedy, still wearing the pink, bloodstained dress, standing beside the casket.

But I saw something else. I saw something that no researcher, no Warren Commission critic, had ever noted. Air Force One did not appear to be Air Force One!

In 1968-69, I had worked on Boeing aircraft during a stint with Western Airlines in Los Angeles. Air Force One was an executive version of the Boeing 707 jetliner. From what I could see, the airplane that transported the Presidential party that day was *not* a Boeing 707. I knew that the government had purchased three 707 derivatives, beginning in the Eisenhower administration, to serve as VIP transports. But this was unlike any 707 I had ever seen. This airplane had something that identified it as being something other than a 707.

It had a ventral fin.

To understand the significance of this, one has to understand that Boeing jetliners built at that time fell into two types: the intercontinental 707, and the shorter range 720 series. Most people have never heard of the 720, even though many have actually been passengers on this type of aircraft without realizing that they were not on a 707. The configurations are so similar that to the non-educated eye, they cannot be identified as being completely different aircraft.

21

The Boeing 707 was the most successful of the first generation of medium long-range jet airliners. It first flew in 1954, and initial versions seated up to 181 passengers. Later versions, such as the 707-320 (which was the airframe purchased by the Air Force for AF-1 and AF-2 and the backup/press plane) could carry up to 195 passengers. The Boeing 720, a shortened version of the same airframe that was limited in range, could only carry up to 153 passengers.

In appearance they look they same with one exception. The B-720, which is 22.5 feet shorter than the 707, has a very large fin that is mounted *under the tail* to compensate for the shortened length of the fuselage. This empennage, known as a ventral fin, only existed on the 720A and 720B versions of the large four-engine transports. Not on the 707.

In both the news footage and in photographs, the airplane delivering Kennedy's body to Andrews AFB—bearing tail number 26000—*was fitted with a ventral fin*. It also mounted four Pratt & Whitney JT3D turbo-fan engines, discernable from earlier version turbojets by their distinctive large, round fan ducts on the front of each engine pod. Therefore, it was configured as a 720 "B" model. The "A" model was fitted with the earlier smooth-cowled turbojets.

I dug into my reference books. I could find no mention anywhere of the Air Force ever owning a 720B. So, if this airplane was indeed what it appeared to be, who *did* own it? And why was it painted in the livery of Air Force One? And more importantly, if it was a forgery, as it appeared, why had it been substituted? Why would a completely bogus airplane have been needed? None of this made any sense. At least not at that time.

Then I came across a remarkable book written by a pioneer critic of the Warren Commission, David Lifton. The book, titled *Best Evidence*, approached the case in reverse of what had been done in the past. This is routine technique for police investigators, considering that we arrive at a crime scene after the event has transpired, and then are forced to reconstruct the crime in reverse. But it is not the norm for researchers and writers. Lifton, investigating the case from the scene of the autopsy at Bethesda backwards to the shooting scene in Dallas, did a wonderful job of research, locating witnesses and procuring diagrams and photographs. Within the pages of *Best Evidence* I found three very important missing pieces of the puzzle. The first was a diagram of the internal layout of Air Force One as it was in 1963. The second was a chronology of events that contained several references to the activities of the aircraft. The third was a description given by Lifton of the sequence of strange events that transpired both aboard AF-1 and afterwards, during the transport of the president's casket to the morgue.

Of particular interest was a notation that a helicopter of some type was running on the right side of AF-1 as it off-loaded the casket at Andrews from the left side, and that this helicopter took off within minutes of the jet's arrival and shutdown. From my past experience in providing security for presidential and vice-presidential VIP visits, I knew that *no* aircraft is allowed within a very strict radius of the presidential aircraft. In fact, no aircraft is permitted to even fly over AF-1 when it is on the ground and the president is aboard, nor is an aircraft permitted within one mile of the presidential motorcade when he is traveling on the ground. Not even his security helicopters. While flying as the advance roof-top scout for then Vice President George Bush during one of his visits, I was told by my Secret Service agent rider that if we got within a mile of the motorcade, they would shoot *us* down! And I later found out that the necessary equipment to do just that was part of the inventory of the security vehicles within the convoy.

So how did *this* machine manage to park right next to the big jet, then be permitted to become airborne? This just did not fit.

The thrust of *Best Evidence* is that the wounds on Kennedy's body had been altered previous to the autopsy. This had to have been done for two reasons: To change or hide the actual entrance and exit wounds to confuse the issue concerning which direction the shots had been fired from, and to remove any evidence that was contrary to the assertion that Oswald fired all the shots and the weapon was his Carcano. It would be very awkward for any conspirators to have particles from other bullets, or worse, other intact missiles found in the body. Lifton's point was that if the body had indeed been altered, then there was a conspiracy. Otherwise, why would it have been done?

If I was correct concerning my observations of the possibility of a bogus aircraft being inserted into the equation, then I might just have the key that would unlock the back door of the mystery. I knew that I had discovered something overlooked by every single researcher, but was my observation completely accurate? I wrote the 89th Airlift Wing at Andrews Air Force Base, which was the command that operated the jets, and requested more information on the history of Air Force One. In the letter, I asked for any photos they had of the aircraft being operated through the years. I wanted to see if any of the official photographs depicted the aircraft with the tail number of 26000, and if so, was it shown with a ventral fin. I also wrote the Boeing Airplane Company in Seattle, Washington, and asked if they had ever produced a 707 derivative with a ventral fin. To this date Boeing has not replied.

Returning to Lifton's book, I read with interest his logical dissertation that the whole investigation was bungled by all involved throughout—especially the autopsy—and the body had been removed from the coffin at some point in time, altered, and only then delivered to Bethesda Naval Hospital for the "official" autopsy. This assertion of events is best summed up by Lifton himself:

"Between the Dallas shooting and the Bethesda autopsy six hours later, President Kennedy's body was secretly removed from the casket. It was then surgically changed. Wounds were altered. Bullets were removed. The body was returned in time for the autopsy—returned as a medical forgery which told a false story of the shooting."[1]

The one thing Lifton was missing in his theory was exactly *where* the body had been altered, and exactly how it could have been removed from the coffin, hidden aboard the aircraft during the trip from Dallas to Washington, removed from the aircraft unnoticed, transported to the site of the alteration, then delivered to Bethesda prior to the arrival of the actual casket—and the media. These were very large gaps that would, under most circumstances, be impossible to fill in. At least for the investigators that were untrained in large aircraft design.

I felt I had the answer. But first I had to wait for a reply to my questions from the 89th Airlift Wing at Andrews.

Within thirty days a package arrived. Inside was a short letter and a large, paperbound book. The book, titled *Historical Highlights Of Andrews AFB; 1942-1989*, contained several grainy photos of various airplanes and a typewritten unit history of the various squadrons and wings that had served at Andrews through the years. The letter was brief and not very responsive to my detailed inquiry.

"Your request for information on presidential aircraft was passed to me, the base Historian," the letter began. "Rather than typing a 20 page response I thought the best approach would be to forward a monograph entitled "Historical Highlights of Andrews AFB." What I had received was the basic brush-off given by public relations officers and other ancillary personnel who are forced to deal with bothersome public inquiries on a routine basis. It was "here's a nice book, so now please go away and leave us alone."

But the paragraph went on a few more lines—one of which *did* answer my main question. "Through research of my archives and in talking with some of the seasoned pilots of the wing I learned that the 720B that you asked about *was never assigned to the 89th* but was told that the C-137B model was often mistaken as a 720B." [author's emphasis].

I turned to the pages bearing photographs of the C-137B to see if the explanation was as simple as that—the C-137B, for some unknown reason, had been constructed with a 720-type ventral fin.

I found no such thing. Instead, the photos showed the typical Boeing 707 configuration. A nice clean tail following the long fuselage of the standard 707-320. Nothing protruded under the tail cone beneath the vertical stabilizer. I could not understand how anyone, even if they *did* know of the existence of the 720B, could mistake this airplane for such an aircraft. I then began to educate myself on just exactly what the Air Force *did* have in inventory in those days.

According to the book, the first Boeing jet *designated* as a presidential aircraft arrived in October, 1962.[2] It was tail number 26000. This aircraft was backed up by a C-137B that "could not keep pace with the President" and was used as "Air Force Two," the vice-presidential and presidential backup aircraft. It was this airplane that carried Lyndon Johnson to Dallas. It would not be until December, 1972 that a third aircraft would join the fleet, tail number 27000.

The Air Force designation for these aircraft was VC-137. The "V" designator was added to indicate VIP type missions. According to the book, tail number 26000 *was* not a "B" model C-137, therefore the explanation that the "B" was often mistaken for a 720B did not apply. And to add to this, a photograph taken on 24 January, 1972, showed this aircraft, tail number 26000, parked on the ramp at Andrews—*and there was no ventral fin beneath the tail!* I sensed an airplane shell-game.

I wrote a second, more detailed letter of inquiry to the 89th MAW. This time, they would not be able to get off the hook quite so easily. As I waited for a reply, I delved into other areas of my investigation.

Chapter 3

Motives For Murder

In almost every instance, there is a motive behind every pre-meditated murder. This may not be the case on every homicide, such as a fight or a thrill killing or other psycho murder, which happens spontaneously, but, for a planned killing, a motive is present. In this case, the motive, for purposes of investigation, could be associated directly to whoever would benefit directly from the death. To address this, a great deal of research was required to ascertain exactly what was going on in the years preceding Kennedy's death.

My research showed, as it did for those who went before me, that the historical events that occurred between 1941 and 1963 correlated directly with the various players—especially those persons and entities that would benefit from the elimination of JFK. Volumes of information concerning the details and background of the events that preceded the assassination are available to those interested. To address them in detail at this time would require a book in itself, and would be a repetition of what has already been covered. Therefore, I will only present the main events and beneficiaries.

Kennedy, by the third year of his term, had made many enemies. Perhaps the most powerful was the Central Intelligence Agency. He had not only refused U.S. air support and the use of a U.S. Marine regimental landing team during the Bay of Pigs invasion, he had ordered the CIA to hold back over half of the air support strike force of Cuban-piloted, CIA provided B-26s from flying in the operation. Without air support, the invasion was doomed to failure. The end result was that Castro's forces managed to surround the beleaguered and stranded invasion force (which was little more than a pre-planned political foothold for a larger, better equipped American force that had been scheduled to follow), before they could advance inland to hopefully be joined by fellow anti-Castro Cubans. The end result was failure of the operation, codenamed "ZAPATA,"[3] and the loss of 120 men killed and 1180 captured by Castro's forces. Besides the human losses, the Cubans captured or destroyed all weapons and material taken ashore, and sank three of the cargo ships in the bay in the process of off-loading. As all of this was transpiring, American pilots, sailors and Marines watched helplessly from the U.S. Navy ships cruising offshore. The "umbrella of air protection" promised by the CIA had been cancelled by the liberal president who was already suspected of being soft on communism. At this point, four potential enemies to the Kennedy regime were born.

The anti-Castro community had lost not only loved ones, but a cause—and a country. The CIA had not only suffered presidential interference in their highest priority operation, causing it to fail, but the leaders of the Agency who were involved were soon after forced to retire, or were fired by Kennedy. The U.S. military was kept out of the action, infuriating the Pentagon planners and field commanders. And finally, the Mafia, who had been forced to flee Havana after Castro's overthrow of Batista, would not have the opportunity to return to the island to recoup their losses. In the three days that Operation ZAPATA was underway, Kennedy's decisions made many enemies, each capable of attempting terminal action against him.[4]

And there was more. Attorney General Robert F. Kennedy had declared war on organized crime and had relentlessly pursued Mafia leaders heretofore neglected by federal law enforcement agencies. This was an extreme embarrassment to J. Edgar Hoover, who instead of fighting interstate organized crime as he was mandated to do, forced his agents to concentrate on individuals and small groups of common criminals which were much easier to catch. Bobby Kennedy demanded that Hoover's agency divert their attentions to a more elusive foe. In the past, Hoover had churned the public relations wheels of the media in an agency-supportive form with such catch phrases such as "the FBI's ten most-wanted list," and "Public Enemy Number One." In reality, the "gangsters" he referred to were representative of small groups of thieves and bank robbers. Seldom did any such organization number over three or four people. The Mafia, on the other hand, numbered in the hundreds. And to make matters worse, had infiltrated so many American cities during and after prohibition, that any campaign against them would be so difficult that Hoover instead chose to ignore their existence. He even stated for record that there was no such thing as the Mafia in America.

Because of this and other reasons, John F. Kennedy chose not to write a Presidential grant of extension that would give Hoover executive exception to his mandatory retirement at age 70, slated to occur on January 1st, 1965. For the first time in his life, Hoover was up against an unsurmountable obstacle.[5] He had good reason to believe nothing would change JFK's mind.

Hoover was only one of the Washington inner-circle old school boys that Kennedy was in the process of removing from office. In the months since he ascended to the presidency, an unusual number of government officials fell by the wayside. Among them were:

* Army Major General Edwin A. Walker, who was fired by Kennedy from his divisional command in Europe because he was too radical—and far too right wing. He left the army to settle in Dallas.

* S. Wesley Reynolds, Secretary Director of the National Security Agency, was fired.

* General Joseph M. Swing, Commissioner of Immigration and Naturalization since 1954, "resigned."

* Assistant Secretary of the Treasury, A. Gilmore Fluse, was forced to resign.

29

* General C. P. Cabell, the brother of the mayor of Dallas, was forced to resign his post as Deputy Director of the CIA. He was a player in the planning of the Bay of Pigs invasion.

* CIA Deputy Director of Plans Richard M. Bissell was forced to resign. He was also instrumental in planning and executing the Bay of Pigs operation.

* CIA Director Allen Dulles, brother of Secretary of State John Foster Dulles, was fired.

* William T. Heffelfinger, 45-year veteran official of the Treasury Department "resigned voluntarily."

* William L. Mitchell, Commissioner of Social Security, resigned.

* Robert Amory, Jr., another Deputy Director of the CIA, was forced to resign after only nine years of service.

* Assistant Secretary of Labor Jerry R. Holleman was forced to resign.

* General Lauris Norstad, six-year commander of U.S. and NATO forces in Europe, was forced to retire.

* Admiral George W. Anderson, a one-term Chief of Naval Operations (CNO), was relieved and replaced unexpectedly.

* Ambassador deLesseps S. Morrison "resigned to run for governor of Louisiana."

* Bobby Baker, Secretary for the Majority and Lyndon Johnson's protege', resigned amidst swarms of charges and denials revolving around illicit activities involving the Mafia,

various politicians and political interests, and the major companies of the defense industry.

* Fred Korth, Secretary of the Navy, who replaced John Connally, was replaced by Kennedy appointee Paul Nitze after problems arising during a Senate investigation concerning government contract awards to particular defense contractors involving Bobby Baker and Lyndon Johnson. Specifically of interest was the TFX (Tactical Fighter Experiment) aircraft that was awarded to General Dynamics of Dallas.

Then came Kennedy's statement that he was going to break the CIA up into a thousand pieces. John F. Kennedy, by this time, had antagonized so many people and entities that it was remarkable that he even ventured out of the White House.

And if all of this were not enough, there was Kennedy's decision to pull all American ground troops out of Vietnam—and the CIA and Special Forces advisors out of Laos.[6] Of particular interest is a document that was written on October 11th, 1963, just a few weeks before Kennedy's death. It was titled *National Security Memorandum No. 263*, and was distributed to the Secretary of State, Secretary of Defense, and the Chairman, Joint Chiefs of Staff. The subject was Vietnam.

"In a meeting on Oct 5, 1963, the President considered the recommendations contained in sections I B (91-3) of the report, but directed that no *formal* announcement be made of the implementation of plans to withdraw 1,000 U.S. military personnel by the end of 1963..."[author's emphasis].

Kennedy planned for an additional 1,000 personnel to be withdrawn each month thereafter until 1965. At that time all U.S. military personnel would have been removed from the country. Kennedy reaffirmed his decision by stating to the media that Vietnam was a war to be fought by the Vietnamese, and that we could not, and would not, fight their war for them.

31

Though his line of reasoning may have been arguably correct, there was a major problem with this decision. A problem that just might have been the motive for murder.

And there were certain people—very powerful people—who began to perceive Kennedy as a threat to their hidden agenda.

Chapter 4

The Profit Factor

In July of 1965, I landed on China Beach, Danang, South Vietnam, with "H" company, 2nd Battalion, 9th Marines. We were the second Marine Battalion Landing Team to land in the Republic of Vietnam, and were soon to become the first to see combat. In my hands I carried a U.S. Rifle, M-14, 7.62mm, gas operated, air cooled, magazine-fed rifle. My particular weapon was made by Winchester. In my squad were other M-14s, but not every one was made by the same manufacturer. Some were built by Remington, some Harrington & Richardson, a few were even International Harvester. There were several sub-contractors that built not only the M-14, but the M-60 machine gun, the M1911A1 .45 automatic pistol, and virtually every other weapon and vehicle purchased by the U.S. Government. Manufacturing weapons and equipment this way had been the standard since World War II. The war in Vietnam would change that practice.

Within eighteen months, the M-14 would cease to be the main battle rifle of every branch of the U.S. military. For by early 1967, it began being replaced by the M-16 rifle, a weapon supposedly "designed specifically for the jungle war in Vietnam."

Originally designed as the AR-10 in 7.62mm by Eugene Stoner of Armalite Corporation, the smaller 5.56mm cousin, designated AR-15, was adopted by the U.S. Army as the M-16. But instead of being mass-manufactured by Armalite, licensing rights were sold to Colt Firearms. And *only* Colt firearms.[7] For the first time since World War II, a single manufacturer became the sole supplier of the main battle rifle of the U.S. military.

I had known of this for years. And I had known that the M-16, instead of being the super-weapon panacea for jungle warfare, was an unreliable piece of junk. Though the original design was good, the selection of caliber and propellant was not. The 5.56mm bullet (.223 caliber), in comparison to the 7.62mm NATO (.30 caliber) round fired by the M-14, could not handle the terrain or ranges of much of Vietnam. The light-weight bullet would not penetrate dense foliage, light fortifications, or even thick bamboo. The M-14 round, on the other hand, could penetrate 1/4" of steel plate. Therefore, if the Vietcong or North Vietnamese troops were behind anything substantial, or were out beyond 350 meters, the maximum effective range of the M-16, they were fairly safe against incoming U.S. rifle fire. The reverse argument we heard at the time was, "but look at all the ammo you can carry." If the bullets you carry won't kill the enemy, then why go to war in the first place?

The shortcomings of the M-16 quickly surfaced and the weapon became a subject of controversy and a long line of investigations. Reports began coming in from the field that dead soldiers and Marines had been found at the scenes of battles with their rifles in various states of disassembly. It was apparent to the investigators that the soldiers had been killed while attempting to clear mechanical jams. Other reports came from live soldiers, some of which wrote their congressmen demanding an explanation on why the most technically advanced country in the world could not produce a weapon that could be relied upon in the heat of battle. One particularly disgruntled soldier said that his M-16 failed to fire at an extremely critical point—just when he had his lieutenant lined up in his sights for the first time in weeks!

Vietnam is known as the Helicopter War. Over 5,000 helicopters were purchased by the U.S. government and shipped to Vietnam. Over

4,000 were destroyed in the course of the war and later replaced. The intriguing aspect of this is that almost all of the helicopters purchased by the U.S. Government during the war were built by one manufacturer: Bell Helicopter of Fort Worth, *Texas*.

In 1965, five light and medium helicopters were in service in Vietnam. They were built by Piasecki, Boeing, Sikorsky, Bell and Hiller. By 1967, almost all light and medium helicopters in country—and all new arrivals—were manufactured by Bell. The venerable UH-1 "Huey" troop transport and the AH-1 "Cobra" gunship, both manufactured by Bell, became the mainstay helicopters of the Vietnam war. It should be noted at this point that a key man in the company who lobbied heavily in favor of Bell receiving favorable treatment by the government was none other than Walter Dornberger, a former Nazi general who had been chief of the German Rocket Center at Peenemunde. Even though he had been convicted of war crimes at Nuremberg, he had managed to escape punishment by being spirited away to this country under a joint Military Intelligence/OSS operation codenamed "PAPERCLIP." The PAPERCLIP operation ignored the past crimes of Nazi scientists in order to recruit them for use by the western powers in the quickly developing Cold War with Russia. (The special prosecutor at the Nuremberg trial was none other than John J. McCloy, who coincidentally later served as high commissioner on the Warren Commission. Both Dornberger, and his scientific colleague, Werner von Braun, were released to the U.S. to work in the aerospace industry).[8]

In 1965, four light vehicles were in service with the various armed forces. These consisted of the American Motors Mighty Mite, the Dodge 3/4 ton "power wagon" personnel carrier, the M-38 Jeep, and the tiny Mechanical Mule. By 1967, with the exception of the vehicles in Marine Corps inventory, all began being replaced by one vehicle: the M-151 1/4 ton truck—made by Ford Motor Company. This was the first time in the history of military procurement of motor transport that all light vehicles being procured came from one manufacturer.

As a final example, we return to the mysterious TFX. The TFX, which was eventually adopte' by the Air Force—after Navy rejection—as the F-111, was an albatross at birth. It was supposed to be designed to fill the dual roles of both multi-use fighter bomber and long range intercepter for the fleet. To fulfill this mission, it had to be able to catapult from, and land upon, aircraft carriers, maneuver at slow speeds at one end of the flight envelope, and then chase bogeys at supersonic speeds at the other. To accomplish this, the design required a variable geometry wing, exceptionally heavy landing gear, and two internal after-burning engines. The result was an ungainly aircraft later nicknamed by pilots as "Aardvark."

The F-111, after being pushed into Air Force inventory by LBJ, had a dismal record of crashes when finally deployed to Southeast Asia. There are several other examples of sole-supplier contracts awarded during this time, but these are some of the premier cases.

It is obvious that a great deal of money went into the bank accounts of selected corporations. The question is, how did these particular manufacturers rate such favorable treatment?

Late in the war in Vietnam, information circulated among the fighting forces that one major stockholder of Bell Helicopter just happened to be a "trust" whose beneficiary was Lady Bird Johnson.[9] This same entity also was rumored to be a major stockholder in General Dynamics of Fort Worth, the builder of the F-111. The M-151 manufacturer, Ford Motor Company, had direct ties to former Ford executive and Edsel proponent Robert Strange McNamara as company president prior to his move to government service as Secretary of Defense under Kennedy and Johnson. A very advantageous position to be in if one is inclined to investments—or taking care of old friends.

And then there was Brown & Root, the huge Texas construction company with ties to LBJ. Brown & Root received the multi-billion dollar contract to dredge Camh Ranh Bay to clear the harbor for deep-draft cargo operations. Even though the protests were loud and long in support of the Vietnamese doing the work in their own country, Johnson made sure that Brown & Root, his major campaign and financial supporters, received the contract.[10]

But an investigation cannot be satisfied with speculation, innuendo and rumors. Even if the above assertions were true, there was still the question of who was making money through Colt Firearms. In an attempt to get to the facts regarding the intricacies of the above corporate structures during the Vietnam years I wrote the Securities and

Exchange Commission in Washington, D.C. In my letter, I asked for information concerning exactly who owned controlling interests, and who were major stockholders in the corporations mentioned above.

Over a period of five months, my letter requesting information was forwarded to various individuals, each promising to send me the information requested "by the end of the week." On two occasions it was "lost," and had to be resubmitted. Finally, I sent a FAX directed to a particular individual that had taken time to call me and say that he had been conducting a routine audit of the correspondence log, and though my letter had been logged in, he could not find any record of it being answered. I informed him that it had not. He asked that I request the information again, and direct the FAX to him personally. My direct question on the FAX was: "Who owned the controlling interest, or was a major stockholder, in the following U.S. corporations between 1960-68: Bell Helicopter, General Dynamics, Colt Firearms, Ford Motor Company, Boeing-Vertol, McDonnell Aircraft, and Douglas Aircraft?"[11]

One week later I received a telephone call from a female assistant to the addressee. In a somewhat mystified sounding voice, she said that she had spent the day looking for the records of the above corporations concerning the dates in question, but had failed to locate them. She said this was most unusual—that those particular records were missing. She went on to say that it was possible, due to the passage of time, that the records may have been transferred to the National Archives. Maybe I should try there.

But before I could write the National Archives, my original letter evidently surfaced at the SEC. On July 29th, 1992, I received a letter with the following statements:

"This is to acknowledge your letter concerning the above referenced. We are unable to provide the information you are in need of because the files *have been disposed* of in accordance with the Commission's Records Control Schedule (17 CFR 200.80f)..." [Author's emphasis].

In a country that archives over 200 years of paperwork, including such important items as World War I memorandums on the procurement procedures for pack mules, World War II technical manuals on obsolete equipment, and records of telephone calls made from various obscure offices during the FDR years, I found it incredible that records dealing with some of the country's corporate giants had been "disposed of." I was disappointed. Another door had been slammed shut by the bureaucracy.

It is obvious that the military/industrial complex was comprised of greedy politicians in public service and industrialists in the private sector. But what about the Mafia? Whenever there is money to be made, organized crime does its best to get a piece of the action. And the big money during the Vietnam years was to be made in the defense industry. For organized crime, one way was a simple matter of doing in the corporate world what they had been doing elsewhere for years: expanding a growing monopoly on vending machines. This foothold in the defense industry arrived in the form of the U-Serv corporation.

Robert G. "Bobby" Baker, LBJ's right-hand man ever since Johnson had served in the Senate, was in business on the side. Baker was in partnership with a Las Vegas casino operative and Mafia money launderer named Edward Levinson in a vending machine company known as the U-Serv corporation. Virtually every large armaments manufacturer in the country that received government contracts leased from U-Serv. If someone received a government contract, it was quietly understood that the employee break rooms and cafeterias would be filled with U-Serv's vending machines.

Levinson was an interesting character himself. He was the brother of Mike and Louis Levinson of Newport, Kentucky, who ran the Mafia gambling operations in one of the wilder towns in the upper midwest at the time. Among his contacts outside of Las Vegas was one Irwin S. Weiner of New Orleans. Weiner worked directly for Carlos Marcello, the New Orleans Mafia kingpin. Levinson's job was to coordinate cash flow between Las Vegas casinos and the Teamsters Union under Jimmy Hoffa. It should be noted at this point that Irwin Weiner was a long-time associate of Jack Ruby. Both had at one time worked for Sam Giancana of Chicago—and through a complicated chain-of-command, still did at the time of the assassination. By charting out associates and connections, it is not difficult to trace an organizational tree that led from the lowest levels of organized crime to the White House.

The end of this particular motive trail can be summed up in one word: Profit. The key is knowing *where* and *when* to invest for war.

When the motives and beneficiaries are combined, it can be seen that several things would occur if Kennedy was eliminated at precisely this point in history: The CIA would remain intact and would be permitted to pursue its operations both world-wide and in Laos; The Mafia, besides making money on the war by way of interests inside the military/industrial complex, and also in illicit drug dealings by distributing the heroin coming out of Laos for the CIA, would be rid of Bobby Kennedy and his anti-Mafia crusade;[12] Life-long high-level government bureaucrats, including J. Edgar Hoover, could keep their jobs; Certain corporate entities—most of which provide financial support to selected politicians, and which do little business in peacetime—would turn billions in profits during a war; The anti-Castro Cuban community would be revenged for Kennedy's treachery during the Bay of Pigs invasion; And lastly, Lyndon Baines Johnson, a nobody vice president—would become President of the United States.

Chapter 5

Levels Of Covert Operation

It was at this stage of my research that I received my second reply from the 89th Airlift Wing at Andrews AFB. This letter was much more detailed than the first, and I read it with interest.

"Let me start by assuring you that there was only one aircraft with the tail number #26000. It was delivered to the 1254th Air Transport Wing on 10 October 1962 as a C-137, (Boeing 707-320). It was originally built with the ventral fin attached but as part of a modification in 1968, the ventral fin was removed. Other modifications included leading edge flaps, new wing tips, take-off flaps from 17-14 degrees, and larger sucker doors. Interior modifications were a result of President Johnson requesting that the stateroom be relocated to the front of the aircraft as well as the entry/exit door."[13]

This explanation, if correct, would explain the lack of a ventral fin on 26000 in the photo taken in 1972. However, it is hard to feature removing such a large structural item during modifications. Such a major alteration would require a complete re-engineering of the tail section structure, new computation of weight and balance of the aircraft, not to mention the reinforcement of the fuselage bulkheads, stringers and other structure and application of new skin. Any benefits from removal of the appendage would be negligible at best. Still, it seemed to be the most logical explanation. The unexplained part is why was this particular 707 fitted with such a fin to begin with? And why no reply from Boeing?

The letter went on: "Aircraft #26000 was the aircraft that transported both President Kennedy and Johnson's body. 6970 did not do this. Although 6970 was used by President Kennedy on several occasions it was never officially designated as the Presidential Aircraft. By the way, no aircraft is called 'Air Force One.' This is only a call sign given to whatever aircraft has the president on board at the time, and 'Air Force Two' is the call sign when the Vice President is on board."

Though this impacted my theory on why there might have been a switch in airplanes, it did not alter the fact that I felt sure I knew exactly what clandestine activities regarding the body had taken place between Dallas and Washington.

And by this time, after painstakingly piecing together other bits and pieces of both known and previously unknown information, I felt I knew what had actually happened *in* Dallas—and who had to have been involved.

In putting the pieces of the 30 year-old puzzle together, one eventually finds—provided the false leads and bogus evidence is identified and cast aside—that only two main entities were required before the fact: The CIA and the Mafia. Certain individuals outside these two organizations would also come into play, but they were hand selected by one or both of the above groups. Ancillary personnel, such as certain anti-Castro Cubans and professional foreign assassins, were also utilized as assets. Their purpose was to provide, if discovered during the investigation, trails that led away from the main participants. To understand exactly who the players must have been, one first must understand the multi-level tiers of the command and control structure of a military-type covert operation. This structure is designed for one purpose: Insulation. The beneficiaries of such an operation, known as a "black" operation—one which, if discovered, is plausibly denied—must be so well insulated from the Action Teams at field level that no one at field level could ever identify (or testify against) anyone at the top. This is done by building an organizational chart in the following manner:

Typically there are three main levels, each insulated by a go-between. The top level, normally limited as much as possible in the number of co-conspirators, consisted of the main planners and those who benefit from a designated activity or action. In this case, they would be top or high level bureaucrats. The initial mission objective is developed at this level, but is passed down to lower levels for detail planning, logistical support, recruiting, key intelligence gathering, and execution.

But the chain of command is not direct. Between the top level and the mid-level is an intermediate contact. This individual, normally working alone, is the only one who knows who to report to on the top level staff. Often he only knows a voice on the telephone, and a codename. A typical assignment might be, "we have a job. It's in Europe. It'll be in the Spring." The intermediate contact (IC), who in this example might specialize in "executive action," or elimination of foreign government officials, understands exactly what this statement means. He only has to wait for further details to pass on to the intermediate level.

The intermediate level normally consists of seven people or less. This level of command is recruited and custom tailored specifically for each mission. A normal staff would consist of a commander (who is the only member in contact with the upstream IC), an executive officer (XO), a personnel officer (S-1),[14] an intelligence officer (S-2), an operations and planning officer (S-3), a logistics and supply officer (S-4), and possibly one or more spares such as a liaison officer from the indigenous population if working abroad. The job of each of these staff members is almost identical to their military counterpart.

The intermediate level staff is responsible for several things. They gather intelligence concerning the operational area, the objective and target, and anything else that would influence the mission. They formulate the plan, recruit the field operational teams (through lower level code-named intermediate contacts), provide logistical support, funding, and transportation if needed, and serve as a conduit of information between the field and the upper level.

Below the intermediate level command staff are one or more code-named contacts who function as direct contact field operative handlers. They also serve, when required, as the field team's command, control and communications, or "C3" (known as "C-cube") element. In this role, they man portable radios, note and broadcast such things as arrivals and departures of the target, and coordinate security and fire control.[15]

In the case of the Bay of Pigs invasion, the CIA instructors and agent handlers who trained the Cubans served the role of ICs between the field forces and the intermediate command staff. These individuals, in the case of the CIA, might be actual CIA agents or "contract" operatives. The code names at this level might only be aliases. As an example, E. Howard Hunt, who worked closely with the Cubans during the preparation stage of Operation ZAPATA, was known simply as "Eduardo." His colleague, Francisco Fiorini, was—and still is—known as "Frank Sturgis."

At the bottom of the chain are the actual operational personnel. These are the individuals or groups that actually perform the mission. In the case of executive action, these teams are made up of either highly-trained cellular teams who operate together on a consistent basis, or individuals that may never have worked together before, and probably will not work together again. The mission dictates either the selection of one of the above courses of action, or a mix-and-match of both. In the case of the Kennedy murder, it was a mix-and-match.

The background of U.S. executive action operations can be traced back to the 1950s, during the years when Fidel Castro came to power. For reasons already discussed, a meld between the CIA and the Mafia came about for reasons of combined interest. The CIA, by virtue of national objectives during the Eisenhower years, wanted Castro eliminated and Soviet influence—and war material—removed from the island located only 90 miles from the American shoreline. The Mafia, which still had many solid contacts inside Cuba (which the CIA did not), wanted to reclaim their casinos and hotels in Havana. It was a natural partnership.

It must be pointed out that the CIA's *Assassination Manual For Latin America*, according to Colonel Fletcher Prouty, former Chief of

Covert Operations for the Joint Chiefs of Staff, states, "If possible, professional criminals will be hired to carry out specific selective 'jobs.'"

In the case of Castro, a CIA operation, codenamed Operation 40, was developed and put into motion. Operation 40 came about under the auspices of the CIA's then super secret "5412 Committee," which was formed to direct covert operations. No actions by field teams could take place without orders, or at least approval, of the committee. The decision makers inside the committee were reportedly Richard Bissell, Deputy Director for Plans and Covert Operations; J.C. King, Director of Western Hemisphere Operations; and Sheffield Edwards, Chief of Security, CIA.[16]

In this instance, the Committee, according to other researchers, contacted none other than Howard Hughes to help set up a front operation for deniability. The Hughes organization assigned former FBI agent Robert Mayheu (who then became an IC) to handle the details. At this point the 5412 Committee passed the ball down to the newly-formed Operation 40 staff (the intermediate level planning staff).

Operation 40, in 1960, was assigned the mission of locating and eliminating Fidel Castro, his brother Raul, and Che Guevara. But the CIA, as mentioned, did not have the assets on hand to accomplish this mission unassisted. Therefore, it was decided to call once again upon the Mafia. The CIA-Mafia connection went back to World War II, when the OSS (Office of Strategic Services, the CIA's predecessor) and the Sicilian and Corsican Mafia worked together in the underground against the Germans. The partnership, though dusty, was still in existence.

Mayheu, serving as the IC at this level, first made contact with Las Vegas mobster Johnny Roselli. Roselli, in turn, contacted the two men who would become key players in providing assets inside of Cuba, Sam Giancana of the Chicago mob, and Santos Trafficante of Miami.

Santos Trafficante had a very personal interest in this operation.

In 1933, the Mafia financial genius, Meyer Lansky, obtained gambling concessions in Cuba. World War II intervened before the mob could infiltrate Cuba in force, but in 1952, after Batista returned to Cuba to seize power after a brief exile, Lansky cut a deal with Batista to allow the mob to establish hotels and gambling casinos.

Among the hotels the mob built, bought or had interests in were the Hotel Nacional, the Sevilla Biltmore and the Havana Hilton. Lansky himself built the Hotel Havana Riviera at a cost of $14 million.

When Santos Trafficante, Sr., died in 1954, his family crime business of narcotics smuggling and gambling fell to his son, Santos Trafficante, Jr. By the end of the decade, Junior was well entrenched in Cuba. He owned a substantial interest in Sans Souci, a famous night spot partially managed by Johnny Roselli, and was in partnership with Lansky in the Tropicana Casino in Havana. This latter property was managed by Dallas gambler Lewis McWillie (Jack Ruby's idol and mentor).

During this time, one distinguished guest in Havana was none other than Richard M. Nixon. Nixon made frequent trips to the island to visit both Batista and the gambling casinos. He even had considered the possibility of establishing a law office, or at least "business connections" in Havana.

When Batista fell during the Communist takeover of Cuba, Castro declared "I'm going to run all these fascist mobsters, all these American gangsters, out of Cuba. I'm going to nationalize everything. Cuba for the Cubans!" By 1960, Castro had expelled organized crime, deported all the syndicate members and closed down the casinos, drug labs and houses of prostitution. The mob and certain U.S. government officials were incensed at these events. Santos Trafficante more than most.

According to various sources, Trafficante was directly responsible for recruiting ten sharpshooters from the Cuban community in Miami for Operation 40's attempt on Castro. The action-team snipers that were selected from this pool were supplied with precision-built take-down Belgian rifles, trained at a secret location known as "The Ranch" in Mexico, then infiltrated into Cuba using CIA assets.[17] Operating under the CIA's executive action program assassination team for the Caribbean and Latin America, codenamed ZR/RIFLE, the Mafia-supplied shooters managed to get very close to accomplishing their objective. But before they could make the hit, they were discovered, arrested, and tortured until they provided the Cubans with the details of the plan.[18]

It is believed that the CIA end of the operation that provided certain CIA ICs and other assets was handled under yet another codename: JM/WAVE. Both Operation 40 and JM/WAVE came under Operation MONGOOSE, the name for *all* operations against Cuba. Though JM/WAVE is mentioned by some sources as being a radio propaganda program utilizing clandestine transmitters in Guatemala, it is more likely that it was actually the CIA end of the Castro operation. The designator JM was the CIA code for the Miami station, which was located on the grounds of the University of Miami.

The plan was a bust, but the organizational structure and key operatives of Operation 40—and ZR/RIFLE—remained intact.

By 1963, John F. Kennedy had not only made enemies who would benefit from his demise inside both government and the mob, but his programs and decisions added other powerful people and entities that would profit if he were to be removed from the presidency. A factor now faced by these entities was the probability that he stood an excellent chance of being re-elected for another term in 1964. If this were to happen, the CIA would cease to exist in its present, powerful form; the Mafia would be pursued in a relentless crusade by the Attorney General's office, (to say nothing of losing millions in drug trafficking profits gleaned from distributing the CIA's opiates coming out of their Laotian operation); Lyndon Johnson was expected to be dropped from the Kennedy ballot in the coming election; The Pentagon would lose "the only war we had;" And finally, certain industries in corporate America would not gain the expected billions in war material profits. One could not ask for a more defined set of suspects and motives.

According to Fletcher Prouty, "After the Bay of Pigs, Kennedy decided he would change the entire structure of how this government would carry out covert operations. He began transferring covert operations directly to the Joint Chiefs of Staff. Shortly after this decision was made, he fired Allen Dulles as Chief of the CIA. That was the signal to the CIA of what Kennedy was going to do next—what he *had* done."

THE KILL ZONE

"Kennedy was changing the *status quo*, from Big Business to the military; from disgruntled intelligence agents to Cubans and their supporters...Kennedy had to go. The mechanism was in place."

Add to this all of the other factors mentioned above and one has more than sufficient motive for murder.

But knocking off a foreign dictator is one thing. Taking out the President of the United States—*inside the country*—is something else. It would be an extremely dangerous prospect at best, a disaster to those concerned if *anything* went wrong. For the conspirators, it must have boiled down to "we may have a great deal to lose if things go wrong, but we have much, much more to gain if things go right." And after all, if the top players are well enough insulated, then the prospect of discovery decreased at every level of the operation.

Due to lack of sufficient hard evidence—since most has long since been altered or destroyed—it cannot be proved beyond all doubt what exactly happened at Dealey Plaza that day. However, by piecing together what we do know from the numerous sources and multitude of references, we can build a picture of such convincing magnitude that there should be no question that the case should be reopened and investigated by proper authorities.

It is now time to reconstruct the crime utilizing what is known, and in some areas, what we can logically speculate must have occurred.

At some point in time, the decision was made to assassinate the President of the United States. This would require, at the top level, only the desire and the authorization for a mission. The mechanics would have to be addressed at the intermediate level.

The actors at the top level, those having the most to gain considering the motives that have been addressed, would have consisted of a meld of selected corporate moguls, high level bureaucrats and politicians, and certain contacts in the covert operations community. Three entities: the money men, the politicians, and the spooks. All were interdependent on each other.

As with the failed attempt on Castro, it was decided to use a combined operation of both CIA and Mafia assets. This decided, in-house personnel were selected for various positions within the command structure, and the same organized crime figures that were used in Operation 40 were contacted through Roselli to provide the majority of the field operatives. By combining eyewitness accounts and information from other sources, the field operational team would consist of professional assassins provided by ZR/RIFLE, the Mafia, and the anti-Castro Cubans. The ZR/RIFLE team members would provide local support, equipment, and intelligence to the first-line shooters—the Mafia-supplied professional assassins and the CIA's anti-Castro Cubans—and if necessary, function as backup marksmen. In case of a miss or malfunction of equipment of any primary shooter, the ZR/RIFLE representative could immediately take over at that particular location with a minimum loss of time.

It should not be assumed that The CIA, as an organization, was involved in this conspiracy. It can only be speculated that certain elements, or individuals within the agency, and certain agency assets, were involved. In the mainstream, the vast majority of CIA personnel had no idea of such an operation being undertaken. This, for the insiders, was easy to accomplish. By their very nature, intelligence organizations are compartmentalized into areas only those with a need to know have access to. No one outside of a given cell will have a clue about what is happening next door. This technique of organization not only provides elements of security, it makes deniability much easier for the organization. It becomes very easy to say, "We didn't know what was going on down there. It was a rogue element operating on its own."

As the plan was being developed, three factors had to be decided: Where, When, and Who. Where would the attempt take place? When would it happen? And who would be involved? Once these questions were answered, back-planning could begin. This is the standard military planning style that approaches a problem in the manner of "if we have to take hill 621 by 0800 hours, then, taking into consideration the time factors, the distance we have to cover, the enemy defenses and strengths, and the transportation and support available, when do we have to initiate the movement phase?"

Back-planning on this particular occasion hinged upon the where, and when. As early as May, two primary operational areas were chosen: Miami, the turf of Santos Trafficante; and Texas, the home state of Lyndon Johnson. Kennedy was scheduled to visit Miami in early November, then Texas later in the month.

In September, 1962, Trafficante made the statement to Jose Aleman, a wealthy Cuban exile living in Miami, that "Kennedy's not going to make it to the election. He's going to be hit." Unknown to Trafficante, Aleman was an informant for the FBI. Aleman reported this conversation to "the Bureau," (read Hoover), but the FBI would either not take him seriously—or suppressed the evidence. The Secret Service claimed they never received the above information.

Then, according to Miami police informant William Somersett, a meeting between him and a wealthy right-wing extremist named Joseph A. Milteer occurred on November 9th, 1963, that gave the second warning to the where and when parts of the original plan. Unknown to Milteer, the conversation was recorded. It concerned Kennedy's upcoming visit to Miami. It went like this:

"...You can bet your bottom dollar he [Kennedy] is going to have a lot to say about the Cubans, there are just so many of them here...the more bodyguards he has, the easier it is to get him."

"How is that?"

"From an office building with a high-powered rifle...He knows he's a marked man."

Somersett then asked, "They are really going to kill him?"

"Oh, yeah. It's in the works. [An investigation] wouldn't leave any stone unturned there. No way. They will pick up somebody hours afterward...just to throw the public off."

But the Miami hit did not materialize. Instead of traveling through the streets of Miami in a motorcade, Kennedy instead flew to the planned function by helicopter.

The next planned ambush zone was Texas.

Chapter 6

The French Connection

Two southern cities served as the main training base headquarters for the anti-Castro Cuban forces trained by the CIA for the invasion of Cuba. Miami, with its large Cuban population and close proximity to huge swamps and wetlands that provided ideal, and secluded, training areas, was the overall headquarters. New Orleans, with nearby Lake Pontchartrain and the northern shore swamps, served as a second base.

In New Orleans, the CIA had two major factors in its favor: The Guy Bannister Detective Agency—a front for gunrunners, mercenary pilots, and transient Cuban soldiers—and the local Mafia kingpin, Carlos Marcello.

Much has been written concerning the connection between Guy Banister and Lee Harvey Oswald. Of note is the link between Oswald's Fair Play For Cuba Committee headquarters at 544 Camp Street, and the Banister Detective Agency at 531 Lafayette Street. Both are addresses located inside the Newman Building, a corner office building that happened to be owned by none other than E. Howard Hunt, "Eduardo" of both Operation ZAPATA and Operation 40 fame. Also seen habitating the premises on occasion was a shady CIA contract pilot named David Ferrie who had flown guns and material to Nicaragua in preparation for the invasion. He also flew loads into Cuba itself on deliveries to anti-Castro guerrilla groups. He surfaces again later.

Carlos Marcello, whose real name was Calogero Miniacore, was a natural-born Sicilian whose family had moved to New Orleans in 1910. As with most mobsters, Marcello joined the Mafia at an early age. By 1947, he had risen through the ranks and become well-established in the race track and gambling casino operations. When his partner, Sam Carolla, was deported back to Sicily in 1947, Marcello took control of Carolla's New Orleans interests. At this time his main national crime contacts were Joe Civello of Dallas (who was close to Jack Ruby), Sam Yaras of Chicago, Mickey Cohen of Los Angeles, and Santos Trafficante who at that time had been identified as Tampa, Florida's, leading mobster.

In the Spring of 1961, Bobby Kennedy was well into his attack on the Mafia—and particularly Carlos Marcello. Marcello, who held an illegal Guatemalan passport, was deported to Guatemala City on the personal orders of RFK. To add insult to injury, Marcello was left at the airport without luggage and almost no cash. However, within a short period of time he was flown back to the U.S. by a Dominican Air Force plane (supplied by the CIA) that was believed to have been piloted by David Ferrie.

Marcello declared war against the Kennedys. Now the opportunity presented to him, via Johnny Roselli and Sam Giancana, to get revenge, was exactly what the doctor ordered. But he couldn't do it alone. And he couldn't do it with his own local resources. They would be too easy to trace, and if caught, he would become immediately implicated. He knew the CIA hierarchy, as with the Castro hit, would be well insulated and disavow any connection with his organization. Behind the scenes, they would also refuse any support in legal defense. But Marcello knew where he *could* turn to for help. He called Santos Trafficante in Miami.[19]

The problem concerning who the Mafia would supply for the hit team was solved by Trafficante. As a veteran in dealing with the covert world of the CIA, he also knew the value of insulation. Instead of using mob hit men, he chose instead to contract the work overseas.[20]

This was not difficult for Trafficanti, for he had long-standing connections with the *Union Corse*, the Corsican Mafia. Within the ranks of that organization were several professional political assassins that had worked for various governments and anarchists through the years. In material discovered by Steve J. Rivele, a Los Angeles reporter and writer, the Corsican Brotherhood provided the out-of-country hit team for the American Mafia.

The principal contact was a former intelligence type turned thug named Christian David, who at one time had even been a contract agent for the CIA. It has been reported that his code name at that time was believed to be WI/ROGUE. He is also believed to have worked with or in the OAS (*L'Organisation de l'Armee Secrete*). During the course of Rivele's investigation, David was interviewed in prison where he is being held for other crimes. He provided the following information.

In May or June of 1963, he had been offered a contract to kill Kennedy by the chief of the Marseille Mafia. He refused to participate, because he felt that the contract would be much too dangerous and would probably fail. He did relate, however, that the contract *was* filled by other persons of his acquaintance.

"There were three killers, all from the Corsican Mafia of Marseille, and they had been hired on a contract placed with the leader of the Corsican Mafia in Marseille, a man named Antoine. Antoine was asked to supply three professional assassins. This he did."

These three were: Sauveur Pironti, Lucien Sarti, and Jorge' Bocognini.[21] By piecing together the statements of various sources, we can build a fairly reliable picture of what happened.

During the Fall of 1963, the three hit men traveled from Marseille to Mexico City where they stayed at a safe house for three to four weeks. It is probable that they actually stayed at the private ranch owned by the CIA where the ZR/RIFLE team was trained and housed. While here, they were briefed and permitted to train. They also met their CIA-ZR/RIFLE counterparts.

After the train-up period, the French-Corsican shooters were transported to Brownsville, Texas, where they crossed the border on Italian passports. They were met on the U.S. side by representatives of the American Mafia out of Chicago (Giancana's people) and driven to Dallas.

In Dallas, they stayed in a CIA provided safehouse to preclude any hotel records of their presence. This house was probably provided by Dallas resident Roscoe White, a CIA operative (codenamed MANDARIN) who was reputed by many researchers to be a member of the ZR/RIFLE assassination team. It is interesting to note that Roscoe White had also been in Lee Harvey Oswald's platoon in the Marines prior to Oswald's "defection" to Russia. It should also be added that Roscoe White was, though a bit stockier, of similar build as Oswald, and to a certain extent, even resembled him. Some photographic experts say that it is White's body that was used in the incriminating photographs depicting Oswald holding the Carcano and political newspaper, *The Worker*, taken outside of his apartment.

While at the safehouse, the Corsican assassins spent several days taking pictures of Dealey Plaza. In the evenings, they, and their ZR/RIFLE counterparts, studied the photos. It was apparent that what was required for the mission to have the greatest chance of success would be a crossfire from three directions. This would require teams of two riflemen each to position themselves in buildings behind the President, and another on the Triple Underpass. But the upper overpass area was quickly vetoed. It would more than likely be crowded with spectators on the day of the visit.

Sarti, according to David, would wear a uniform. He would not elaborate, but said that they were always in disguise. "If there is a military base nearby, they wore military uniforms." This particular piece of evidence becomes very valuable later.

While all of this was taking place, another group was entering the picture. Enroute from their main base in Miami were six more players. Riding in two cars in convoy, according to a deposition given to Washington lawyer and assassination researcher Mark Lane, by Marita Lorenz, were MONGOOSE/ZAPATA veterans "Frank Sturgis," two Cuban brothers named Novo,[22] a Cuban pilot named Pedro Diaz Lanz, and Lorenz. Lorenz was Fidel Castro's former girlfriend, who had been recruited by the CIA in another assassination attempt, this time to poison the dictator. But she had failed and subsequently fled Cuba to work for the CIA full time.

In the deposition, Lorenz testified that the five persons named traveled to Dallas from Miami in two cars, one of which contained several weapons in the trunk. When asked if she was told what the purpose of the trip was, she answered that Sturgis told her it was "confidential." During the course of the testimony, which was later used in a defamation lawsuit against a Washington publication which Lane was defending, she stated that they had arrived in Dallas a few days before the assassination, and had checked into a motel. Mr. Lane's questions were followed by shocking responses:

"Q. While you were at the motel, did you meet anyone other than those who were in the party traveling with you from Miami to Dallas?

A. Yes.

Q. Who did you meet?

A. *E. Howard Hunt.*

Q. Was there anyone else who you saw or met other than Mr. Hunt?

A. Excuse me?

Q. Other than those?

A. *Jack Ruby.*

Q. Tell me the circumstances regarding your seeing E. Howard Hunt in Dallas in November of 1963.

A. There was a prearranged meeting that E. Howard Hunt delivered us sums of money for the so-called operation that I did not know its nature.

Q. Were you told what your role was to be?

A. Just a decoy at the time." [author's emphasis]

But instead of being a decoy, Lorenz became frightened at what was transpiring and made Sturgis/Fiorini take her to the airport to catch a flight back to Miami. When asked when this meeting took place in relation to the assassination of the president, she responded, "The day before."[23]

THE KILL ZONE

By the evening of the 21st of November, the field operational team had assembled and readied their equipment for action. The next day would begin early. Security personnel would have to be in place to secure the shooting positions from public access. Communications personnel and those charged with reporting the progress of the motorcade would be in position, and finally, the marksmen would move into their planned "hides."

Early in the morning, the scout elements, driving various cars, drove through and around Dealey Plaza. One car, a mud-splattered Chevrolet, was spotted by railroad worker Lee Bowers from his position in the railroad control tower north of the parking lot on the Grassy Knoll. He later remembered a man driving slowly around the parking lot as if looking it over, speaking into a radio microphone, then driving away.

The operational zone cleared, the security teams moved in to cordon off the areas to be used by the shooters. Each carried bogus identification showing him to be something he was not: Secret Service, Dallas police, and FBI.

Finally, the area secured, the shooters arrived. Each moved casually to his respective spot. Roscoe White and Lucien Sarti took up their positions behind the picket fence on the Grassy Knoll. Either Roscoe White was wearing a Dallas police uniform—he had been employed by the DPD on November 5th to work as a photographer while awaiting a slot in the Dallas Police Academy—or he had lent one to Sarti who "always wore a uniform or disguise" as part of his method of operation when working abroad.

Bocognini and Pironti, each backed up by a control agent with a radio, settled in to their spots at the east end of the plaza. One was on the roof of Dallas County Records Building, where he cradled a .30-06 rifle loaded with a very special ammunition; the other was on a fire escape on the Dal-Tex building, only a little above ground level.

Three other riflemen, all from the Cuban-ZR/RIFLE segment—probably consisting of the two Novo brothers and one CIA intermediate contact agent—took up their diversionary positions *on the sixth floor of the School Book Depository*. One man, spotted by witness Carolyn Walther, who was standing on the east side of Houston Street, was described as being a white male with either blond or light colored hair, wearing a white shirt. He was standing at the western-most window holding a short rifle. She also said that there was a second, heavy-set man wearing a brown suit standing just to his left. The barrel of the rifle was pointed at a downward angle, in the direction from which the motorcade would come: Houston Street.

Another man, described by other witnesses, stood in the far *eastern* window of the depository. He was described as a dark-complected Cuban, or possibly a negro.

All of the shooters were now in place.

Chapter 7

Into The Kill Zone

Early that morning, Lyndon Johnson and JFK had a tremendous argument in their Fort Worth hotel regarding who was going to ride with whom when they reached Dallas. LBJ insisted that Texas Governor Connally ride with him in his Cadillac, and Senator Ralph Yarborough ride in Kennedy's Lincoln. Kennedy vetoed that and finally told Johnson that Connally was going to accompany *him,* and Johnson would have to accommodate Yarborough—a man LBJ despised.

Now there, it was too late to notify the field action teams already set up overlooking Dealey Plaza that the target positions had been altered at the last minute. If Yarborough was on the target list, he was no longer positioned riding in front of Kennedy.

Instead of driving across the metropolitan area to the Trade Mart in Dallas, Kennedy chose to fly the short distance. This way he would not have to drive past the General Dynamics plant where LBJ's F-111 was being developed.

It had rained that morning, but the sky was clearing as the presidential party de-planed at Dallas Love Field. Enthusiastic crowds lined the streets as the motorcade made its way through the downtown area. Finally, it came to the right-hand turn that swung from Main street onto Houston.

The convoy slowly moved north on Houston until it reached Elm. At that point, the lead vehicle, driven by Dallas police captain P.W. Lawrence, turned left, almost coming to a stop as it negotiated the 120 degree turn. Lawrence was followed by a backup car carrying Deputy Chief G.L. Lumpkin, Detective Chief F.M. Turner, Lt. Col. G.L. Whitmeyer, Detective B.L. Benkel, and Kennedy aide J.L. Puterbaugh. This car was followed by eight motorcycles riding four abreast, then the car in which rode Dallas Chief of Police Jesse Curry, Secret Service agent Winston Lawson, Dallas County Sheriff Bill Decker, and Secret Service agent Forrest Sorrels.

Then came the dark blue Lincoln.

Arnold Rowland and his wife, Barbara, were standing on Houston Street across from Dealey Plaza. For some reason, Arnold looked up at the Book Depository and detected movement on the 6th floor. At the easternmost window, he noted what he described as a dark-skinned man who appeared to be "an elderly Negro." Then, running his eyes along the floor to the *western* end of the same floor, he spotted another man. This one, described as a white male, clasped a rifle across his chest in what is described in the military as "port arms." He was standing a bit back from the window, like he was waiting for something.

Arnold directed Barbara's attention to the depository. But by the time she looked up, the man with the rifle had faded back into the shadows. Thinking that the sharpshooters were Secret Service agents, both turned their attention back to the approaching motorcade.

Amos Euins, a sixteen year-old student, was standing on the corner of Houston and Elm where the street made the 120 degree turn to the west. As the president's blue Lincoln slowed to negotiate the turn, Euins waved briefly and then happened to look up at the Depository. He later testified before the Warren Commission that he had seen "a pipe" sticking out of a window. The window with "the pipe" was the easternmost window on the sixth floor.

The western end of Dealey Plaza, near the Grassy Knoll also had been the subject of some strange happenings. Gordon Arnold, a 22 year-old soldier on leave from basic training, had taken his mother's movie camera to Dealey Plaza to film the activities.

"I walked to this particular corner [near the railroad bridge] because I wanted to take pictures off the railroad bridge. But just as I started to cross [a horizontal pipe barrier that was crotch high] a man came around the corner of the bridge, who had a suit on, and he told me I wasn't going to be there. I told him 'you and who else is going to keep me off the bridge?'"

"He pulled out an identification card and said 'I'm with the *CIA*.' I said, 'well, that's enough muscle. I'll leave.'"

"I turned around and walked down the fence line about halfway and was looking over the fence to see if I could get a good shot of the parade, and he came back up and told me 'I told you to get out of this area!' I said, 'okay,' so I walked the complete length of the fence, and got around on the other side.

"That is when I started to line up my frame so I could take a picture of the parade." Arnold began panning his camera in the direction of the 120 degree turn just as the motorcade began to make the turn.

Through the accounts of these and many other eye witnesses, the Zapruder film, still photos, reports, documents and various publications of note, what happened next can be reconstructed with a great degree of accuracy. This is not the same reconstruction demonstrated in the Warren Report, but one that takes into account the relevant facts that have been related by witnesses and evidence never called before the Warren Commission. Much of the evidence and testimony available at the time, though available to the Commission, was, for what appear to be reasons of deception, purposefully not presented by the Warren Commission's "investigators."

What follows is a reconstruction utilizing a logical meld of the evidence:

As the Lincoln entered the kill zone—the section of street where the firing trajectories of all sniper positions intersected— the order was given to commence firing.[24] From behind the picket fence, the first marksman squeezed his trigger. His shot, an underpowered round loaded specifically to stun the target and at the same time present a subdued sound signature, struck Kennedy in the throat. This shot entered the president's neck near the knot on his neck tie, grazing it before penetrating his shirt. Because of the low velocity of the round, the bullet did not penetrate deeply or become what is known in forensic ballistics terminology as a "through-and-through gunshot wound."

In the Zapruder film, Kennedy can be seen emerging from behind a large metal freeway sign clutching his throat with both hands as if he were choking. His face bore a look of surprise. Jackie is also seen at this point beginning to notice something wrong with her husband. It is possible that this shot was fired by a small caliber rifle—probably a CIA-issued .22 caliber Model 74 Winchester silenced sniper rifle—to immobilize Kennedy's head for the high powered rifle shots to come later.[25]

One of the two Grassy Knoll shooters, possibly Roscoe White, was the technician on this shot.[26]

As the Lincoln slowly approached Abraham Zapruder's position on the steps of the monument, a second shot was fired. This shot, however, came from the Dal-Tex building located to the rear of the president, across from the Texas School Book Depository. It was also an undercharged cartridge, for after striking Kennedy in the back, 4" below his collar and just to the right of his spine, it failed to penetrate more than one inch. It later was either clandestinely removed, prior to the arrival of Kennedy's body at Bethesda, or fell out sometime after the motorcade raced away from the kill zone. This hit was also not a through-and-through gunshot wound, as later described by Commission attorney Arlen Specter and upheld by the Warren Commission.

Kennedy's body slumped forward slightly, but not dramatically as it would if struck by a high velocity rifle round such as the 6.5mm Carcano supposedly used by Oswald. Instead, Kennedy merely dropped his head down slightly and leaned forward a few inches. Governor Connally, in the film, can be seen turning around at this point to see what was happening behind him. He looked at Kennedy, then—even though this shot came from behind—turned his head back forward to look at the Grassy Knoll. It is obvious that at this point Connally is unharmed. The Warren Commission, however, maintained that this shot went through Kennedy's back, just below and to the right of his neck, exited his throat near his necktie, then struck Connally, leaving seven wounds in two men. This presentation of disinformation created by Specter to explain how so many wounds were made by the three bullets fired by "Oswald" was later dubbed "the Magic Bullet Theory" by critics. The most bizarre point on this particular shot, if one believes this theory, was that the bullet had to make two 90 degree turns between Kennedy's body and Connally, and had to pause 1.8 seconds in flight at the same time.

The next shot was fired from the School Book Depository and is the actual shot that struck Connally. It penetrated his back, traveled around his rib cage, breaking a rib, then exited his chest near his right nipple to strike his right wrist, which held his white Stetson hat. It then deflected downward into his left thigh. Connally, obviously shocked that he, too, had been hit immediately screamed, *"My God! They're going to kill us all!"*

The next shot came from the Dal-Tex building, fired as a diversionary shot that narrowly missed the limo. It flew long and struck the curb near the triple underpass and shattered into fragments. One such fragment ricocheted up to hit James Tague, a bystander who was standing between Main and Commerce streets, on the right cheek.

The fifth and sixth shots were fired almost simultaneously. The fifth shot came from the Book Depository—possibly from the roof—and also missed the car. It struck the sidewalk on the north side of the street to the right of the limo, leaving its mark in the cement.

At this time, for some unknown reason, the presidential limousine—instead of racing away from the scene as was procedure—came almost to a stop. Witnesses reported that the brakelights came on briefly and Agent Greer (the driver) and Agent Kellerman turned around to look at their passengers. The limousine was now positioned exactly at the intersection of fire from the three points of triangulation.

The sixth, and final shot, would not miss. It was the one fired by a man positioned behind the picket fence, approximatley 30-40 feet west of the corner of the fence on the Grassy Knoll.

As so vividly portrayed in the Zapruder film, this shot struck Kennedy in the right front temple area of his head and exploded on contact. His head was instantly driven to the left rear. Pieces of brain, skull and blood spurted from the rear of the President's head and struck a Dallas Police motorcycle officer riding escort to the left rear of the limo. Other bits of skull and brain matter from the President's right temple explode in a vertical plane—not a conical pattern cast forward as alluded to by the "rear head shot" advocates. The film plainly depicts a reddish mist that casts a piece of skull directly *upwards* at a 90 degree angle to the ground. Such a bullet strike can only be accomplished by an exploding—or "frangible"—bullet. The type of bullet favored by Lucien Sarti.

Almost immediately, Jackie, after recoiling in horror, crawled out of the seat, crossed the trunk lid on her hands and knees, and retrieved a piece of JFK's skull. It was later found still clasped in her gloved hand at the emergency room at Parkland.[27]

At this point the limousine, now bearing the fatally wounded president, finally accelerated away from the kill zone.

Beyond the triple underpass, commanding a direct line-of-sight view of the Grassy Knoll and picket fence *from the rear*, stood a very important witness to what had just happened. Ed Hoffman, a deaf mute, through sign language, later described what he had witnessed.

"...I focused in on a gentleman with a suit and a hat at the picket fence. I saw a puff of smoke, and a man with a rifle...I was shocked. It was a brown rifle. I saw the man with the suit and the hat pitch the gun to the 'railroad man' in this direction."

Hoffman reenacted what he saw for a video documentary filmed in the 1980s. For the camera, he posed behind the picket fence as if holding a rifle, then walked casually but quickly along the fence to the west where he pantomimed throwing the "rifle" to another man. He then turned, adjusted his invisible hat, and walked away toward the east end of the fence. At that point he stopped this activity and moved to the west end of the fence to portray the man who received the rifle. He explained that this man was dressed like a railroad worker. He made motions of breaking the rifle down, placing it in a tool box or tool bag, then, carrying the invisible box, walked to the north along the railroad tracks toward the parked box cars.

Gordon Arnold, the young soldier who had just come out of basic training where he had been subjected to being in close proximity to various forms of small arms fire, and who was standing in front of the picket fence throughout the activity, related what had happened directly behind him on the Grassy Knoll—from behind the picket fence.[28] "A shot came right past my ear [from behind]...A second shot was fired over my head!"

At this point Arnold hit the ground, still clutching his mother's movie camera.

"...While I was laying on the ground, a gentleman came up from this direction [picket fence behind Arnold], and I thought he was a police officer because he had the uniform of a police officer. But he didn't wear a hat, and his hands were dirty.[29]

"Literally what the man did was kick me and ask me if I was taking pictures. I told him that I was, and when I looked at the weapon [he held in his hand]...I decided I would go ahead and let him have the film. Three days later I was in Alaska and didn't come back to the U.S. for eighteen months."

Numerous other witnesses abound that place assassins on the Grassy Knoll. Indeed so many that the majority of witnesses in the Plaza, including the police officers and sheriff's deputies, raced toward that spot as soon as they could cross the street. Others, who had been standing nearby, can be seen on the movie footage taken at the time to be hugging the grass in fear.

But diversions were taking place. Police officers who managed to run up the hill and race behind the fence, and who obviously ran directly into one of the assassins—the man in the brown suit—were surprised when the man showed them the credentials of a Secret Service agent. Citizens were directed to "stay back" by a "uniformed Dallas police officer." At this point in time, the three-man team on the Knoll had performed flawlessly. The rifle, hidden inside the tool box, was now disappearing into the railroad yard. The two shooters, instead of trying to immediately escape, briefly joined in the hunt before disappearing.[30]

Meanwhile, the Book Depository team made its escape down the stairs to one of the three floors below—above the 2nd floor where too many employees, including Lee Harvey Oswald, lingered—and hid out long enough for the building to become inundated with police and news reporters. At that point, in the confusion created by the mob that began to fill the building, they made their escape out of the back door, each going a separate way. One, described by Randolph Carr, a steel worker who was employed nearby on construction site of the new courthouse building, was a heavy-set white man with horn rimmed glasses and a tan sport jacket. He had earlier spotted this very same man on the 6th floor of the Depository. Carr followed the man for about a block and witnessed him get into a light colored Nash Rambler station wagon which quickly sped away.

Within minutes the Depository was overwhelmed with police, all racing up to the 6th floor. Three expended 6.5mm shell casings had been found, laying side-by-side only a few inches apart next to the open southeast window, and a hunt began in earnest for a weapon. Roger Craig, a distinguished Deputy Sheriff who had been Officer of the Year in 1960, described the search.

"We began the search for a weapon. Deputy Sheriff [Eugene] Boone and myself just happened to head for the northwest corner of the building. Boone was ahead of me by about eight feet. There were a stack of boxes just at the head of the stairwell going downstairs [the only route of escape]. Boone looked over into it and said 'Here it is! Here's the rifle!'"

"I immediately walked over beside him and looked, and there was this rifle. But we didn't touch it until after Captain Fritz and Lieutenant Day of the Dallas Police Department [came over]. Now, Captain Fritz was chief of the Homicide Bureau, and Lieutenant Day was from the Identification Bureau. Now they got there and took some pictures of the rifle, then Day pulled the rifle out and handed it to Captain Fritz who held it up by the strap. He asked if anyone knew what kind of rifle it was. Deputy Constable Seymour Wietzman joined us. Weitzman was a gun buff. He had a sporting goods store at one time and was very good at weapons. He said 'It looks like a Mauser,' and he walked over to Fritz, and Captain Fritz was holding the rifle up in the air, and I was standing next to Weitzman, who was standing next to Fritz, and we weren't standing any more than six or eight inches from the rifle. And stamped right on the barrel of the rifle was *7.65 Mauser*!"

"That's when Weitzman said 'It *is* a Mauser,' and pointed to the 7.65 Mauser stamp on the barrel."

"The shells we found came from a 6.5 Italian carbine."[31]

Jim Garrison, former New Orleans District Attorney, points out in his book, *On The Trail Of The Assassins*, that a *third* rifle had surfaced immediately after the ambush. This particular weapon, also a Mauser, had been discovered on the *roof* of the Depository. In a film taken by an independent film company, the Dallas Cinema Associates, police officers are shown gingerly carrying the rifle down a fire escape. When the camera zooms in for a close-up, the legend "The Assassin's Rifle" appears at the bottom of the screen. The intriguing thing about this particular weapon was the fact that it did not mount a telescopic sight.

Both of these rifles quickly disappeared. Only the "Oswald" Mannlicher-Carcano remained in police custody by that evening.[32]

Three other very mysterious events occurred at precisely the time of the incident that cannot be explained as simply coincidence. First, the Washington telephone system was jammed into uselessness for almost an hour, effectively shutting down all communications between government offices and the outside! Second, for some unexplained reason, all code books aboard the airplane carrying the U.S. congressmen and senators to Japan for a meeting concerning world affairs and the situation in Vietnam were missing. This in itself was a very serious matter. For without the code books, no messages could be encoded, or more importantly, decoded, concerning matters of national strategic importance—such as the assassination of the president. On this day, these code books were were missing from the cockpit radio compartment.

Lastly, one of the motorcycle microphones in the motorcade stuck in the "on" position, effectively cancelling all Dallas police radio communications on that frequency for the entire time of the ambush. This, however, would later come back to haunt the conspirators—and the Warren Report.[33]

As confusion reigned in Dealey Plaza and the Book Depository, the presidential Lincoln arrived at the emergency entrance at Parkland. Both the wounded president and Governor Connally were quickly rushed inside to trauma rooms where teams of doctors that were highly experienced in extreme trauma—gunshot and knife wounds—immediately began medical procedures in an attempt to save their lives.

Dr. Charles Crenshaw, a resident physician at the time who was in the trauma room containing the President, explained what he had witnessed during the initial examination.

"I saw evidence of two wounds that came from the *front*. The head wound was tangential in nature, but was a large [open] area in the right rear part of the head. There was a loss of part of the parietal, temporal, and most of the occipital lobe of the right cerebral hemisphere, with exposure of the cerebellum.

"It was about 2 1/2" to 2 3/4" in diameter, more or less circular in shape, and had the appearance of an exit wound. When I saw the autopsy photos [later], there was no damage, or *no* wound in the right rear area.

"The second wound that I saw from the front was the anterior neck wound, which was from 3-5mm—or less than 1/4" in diameter. It was clearly demarcated, round, and relatively clean cut. When the endotracheal tube didn't work, Dr. [Malcolm] Perry performed a tracheostomy through the entrance wound [throat]. The incision was sharp, with smooth edges 1" to 1 1/2" long. I might add it was the same when the tube was removed *before* he was put into the coffin.

"But the autopsy photos showed a wide gaping wound with serrated edges about *three to four inches long*.

Though the doctors at Parkland worked intensely to save the President's life, there simply was too much traumatic damage. He was declared dead twenty minutes after arrival.

Since there were no federal laws that addressed murder, nor were there federal statutes concerning assassination of the President of the United States at the time, Texas law had complete—and the only—jurisdiction in the case. What happened after the President expired was indeed bizarre. As preparations were being made to move Kennedy's body to the Parkland morgue for autopsy, as dictated by the law concerning homicide victims in Texas, a group of Secret Service agents intervened. In a very loud and menacing manner, they threatened the pathologist and other personnel in the hallway outside of the trauma room, arguing over who would take custody of the body. They then forcibly removed the bronze-colored ceremonial casket from the hospital and transported it to Love Field where it was unceremoniously loaded aboard Air Force One. For some reason, someone did *not* want the body to be autopsied in Dallas.

Chapter 8

Oswald, Tippit, And The Dallas Police

As the president was being rushed to the hospital, the assassins were busy breaking contact. The French-Corsican assassins, each taking advantage of the confusion at the scene, made their separate ways out of the area. According to Christian David, they met at the safehouse where they stayed holed up for ten days while the heat died down in Dallas. Even after Oswald was killed by Ruby, they continued to hide until they felt it safe to travel. They were then flown to Montreal (probably by David Ferrie) in a private plane. In Montreal they were met by established contacts who provided transport back to Marseille.

Later, the three foreign assassins—Sarti, Bocognini and Pironti—met in Buenos Aires where they were paid for their part in the ambush in heroin. They then converted this heroin into cash through a Corsican Mafia contact named Michelle Nicole'. The heroin, it is believed, came from the American Mafia, supplied by their CIA connections in Laos and the Golden Triangle. According to underworld sources, Sarti and Bocognini stayed in South America in the drug trade, but Pironti returned to France. Sarti later moved to Mexico City, and was murdered there in 1975.

According to Nicole', Sarti always used an explosive, or frangible, bullet. He stated "it explodes on contact, makes a larger hole in the body, and it is hard to trace because of fragmentation. It self-destructs." David said that Sarti was the only one he knew that used this type of bullet on jobs. This is exactly the description of the fatal bullet that struck Kennedy's head, and left only particles scattered throughout his brain.

According to Marita Lorenz, the CIA people in involved in the operation left Dallas and traveled clandestinely to a ranch in Mexico to hide out until after Christmas, whereupon they returned to Miami. Later, Frank Sturgis bragged to her that she had missed "the really big one," that "We killed the President that day. You could have been part of it—you know, part of history. You should have stayed. It was safe. Everything was covered in advance. No arrests, no real newspaper investigation. It was all covered, very professional."[34]

The "ranch" referred to was probably the ZR/RIFLE facility in Oaxaca, 321 miles southeast of Mexico City. Here, according to one informant, 25-30 professional assassins were trained and housed. These gunman, according to the source, were issued Mauser-type bolt action rifles. The facility was reportedly run by a character named Albert Alexander Osborne, also known as John Howard Bowen. Osborne, as a cover, posed as a missionary with the American Council of Churches. After the assassination, Osborne "disappeared" forever.[35]

But what about Lee Harvey Oswald? Oswald, though part of the operation, unknowingly had been selected as a diversion. In his own words he exclaimed to the press that he was a "patsy."

Entire books have been written describing Oswald's past and links to the intelligence community. Some say he was recruited by the CIA, others the FBI and still others, the KGB. The most logical assumption is that Oswald was originally ONI—Office of Naval Intelligence. He was recruited while stationed at Atsugi, Japan, as a Marine radar operator working air traffic control. Atsugi was an operational center for "spook" operations such as the U-2 spyplanes that overflew China and Russia. Sometime during his tour he, along with Roscoe White, was recruited by the intelligence community, and sometime later—probably just before "defecting" to Russia—he became a shared asset.[36]

According to Victor Marchetti, Deputy Assistant to the Director of the CIA, Richard Helms, "Oswald was likely a 'dangle,' an American intelligence agent put out there for the Soviets to recruit in the hope that he could penetrate the Soviet intelligence network. [He probably worked for] the Office of Naval Intelligence, the Navy's CIA."

Regarding Oswald's status at the time of his defection to Russia, Marchetti said, "I believe Oswald was working with Naval Intelligence, but the FBI was coordinating on the operation, as was the CIA when he was in Russia."

What is known is this: Oswald had a CIA "201" file. A 201 file is a personnel file which contains all records regarding an employee. In Oswald's case, his 201 file took up two entire file drawers. He also had an FBI registered informant number, S-179, and drew a monthly paycheck from the Bureau of $200.00.[37]

It appears that Oswald felt that something had gone wrong by the time the police and media stormed the Depository. He had been quietly having a soda in the break room when accosted by a Dallas officer. When identified as an employee, the officer charged off to search the next floor. Oswald then left the building, but instead of being picked up as would have happened in a planned escape, he departed on foot. Then instead of disappearing in what would have been a normal escape plan, he went to a room he had rented and supposedly picked up his .38 Smith & Wesson revolver.

According to the Warren Commission, Oswald then left the room and began walking through the neighborhood. Then, for some reason, Dallas officer J.D. Tippit is said to have stopped him for questioning. Oswald supposedly shot Tippit, then escaped only to reappear shortly thereafter outside the Texas Theater. The problem with this assertion is that the shell casings found at the scene of Tippit's slaying were from two separate pistols, one of which was a .38 *automatic*. And a revolver, such as that owned by Oswald, does not eject shell casings when fired. Also, an eye witness to the killing, Acquilla Clemons, stated that *two* men killed Tippit, neither of which matched Oswald's description. But she was never called to testify, and indeed, was told by men she assumed to be plainclothes policemen (because they carried guns) to forget what she had seen or "she might get hurt."

Oswald, even though he had money in his pocket, went into the Texas Theater without buying a ticket. Because of this, the police were called. In a bizarre show of force for a "no pay" call, 28 police officers converged on the scene to take Oswald into custody. It was at this point that Oswald must have known for sure that he had been duped. For at that very moment the plan did not fall into place as he had been led to believe.

According to Johnny Roselli, who divulged the information just prior to his own murder, Oswald was to have been met at the Texas Theater by a contact who would take him to a local airport. There, he would be flown to either Mexico or Central America where he would "disappear." The actual plan was to take him out of the country and kill him. He would be identified as the assassin of the president, and a world-wide manhunt would ensue. It is probable that his body would be quickly found, then presented as "shot attempting to escape apprehension." An alternate plan would be to identify the assassin, then discover that he had fled to Cuba. This later plan would serve several purposes, not the least of which would be to implicate Castro in the murder.

However, instead of meeting his contact at the theater, he was apprehended by the police as the cop killer who shot Tippet. It will probably never be known exactly why Tippit was shot. It may have been part of an elaborate plan to add credibility to Oswald's desperate escape, or even part of a Machiavellian plot to leave false trails, assumptions and conjecture to hide the true facts. If this was the case, it served its purpose well.

Whatever the reason, Oswald was now in the custody of the Dallas police Homicide Bureau. He was held and interrogated for sixteen hours over a period of 72 hours—without a single report being made of the proceedings, without notes being taken, with no stenographer present and no recordings of any type made.[38]

What *did* happen during this period is the entrance of Jack Ruby. Ruby, the local night club owner and former bag man for Al Capone in Chicago, had a spiderweb of connections to organized crime. He was directly associated with Carlos Marcello, Lewis McWillie, Johnny Roselli, Sam Giancana and Santos Trafficante. It is not hard to comprehend just how Ruby entered the picture. In the words of one mobster, "If the mob tells you to make a hit, you make a hit. That's it. You ain't got no choice."

And Ruby was told to hit Oswald.

Chapter 9

Shell Games On Air Force One

After the coffin bearing the dead president was placed aboard Air Force One, the coverup entered its second stage (the first began with framing Oswald and ended when the casket was forcibly removed from Parkland).

It is at this point that David Lifton, in his work, became unable to explain the Dallas-Washington shell game played with the body. For the first time in the long history of assassination investigations an explanation of what had to have happened will now be presented.

The bronze casket was carried up stairs to the back entry way of the airplane and placed on the floor just inside the door. It was positioned fore-and-aft on the left side of the area just in front of the hatch. On Air Force One (26000) at the time of the incident, the interior configuration was thus: Inside the tail cone of the fuselage was the auxillary power unit compartment. This APU provided on-board electrical power to the aircraft that was independent of ground-supplied power. Moving forward from the APU compartment bulkhead are two toilet compartments similar to those found on commercial jetliners. Next, on the right, is a closet. Then, taking up the space between the toilets and the bulkhead of the presidential bedroom, was the small room which contained the aft galley and the casket. Moving forward from this point could only be done along the left side of the aircraft. A single aisle ran along the left side, along the bedroom longitudinal wall, to the center of the airplane just over the wings. This area was the Presidential Stateroom which contained a sofa, a table and the President's desk. Beyond this point, and another wall, was the Press and Staff area, and finally the Crew's Quarters, Forward Galley, Communications Compartment, and cockpit.

The only way anyone could see the casket from the Stateroom area was if they purposely looked down the aisle that ran beside the Bedroom to the Aft Galley—provided the curtains had not been drawn shut.

It is at this point that previous authors have run into problems trying to explain how, if Kennedy's body was removed from the casket and hidden somewhere for a later clandestine off-loading, such a feat could occur.

As soon as I saw a diagram of the interior of AF-1 (26000), provided in *Best Evidence*, I knew how it must have been accomplished. It is only because I used to work on Boeing 707s that I had the missing clue. But to be positive, I pulled my old 707 maintenance guides from my library archives and opened them to the cutaway diagrams of the aircraft.

I was right.

Just to the right of where the casket was placed is a trap door that drops down into the aft baggage compartment! It is no secret that the door, known as the "Aft Cargo Compartment Ceiling Access Panel," exists. Diagrams of every access panel and every hatch and door of the airplane are in every maintenance manual. The general knowledge of the existence of this particular access point, however, is not apparent as it is hidden beneath the carpet.

In my theory that a different airplane had been substituted—the 720B I originally questioned—I felt that the reason was because the aft baggage compartment had been specially prepared in advance to receive the body, and if so, probably had the facilities to alter it. The compartment, accessible from the main passenger compartment above, is heated, air conditioned, pressurized and lighted. Animals are often carried in both fore and aft compartments in cages, and therefore must have the same life-sustaining capability as the passenger compartment.

74

THE KILL ZONE

But if what the 89th Airlift Wing said was true—the aircraft had been delivered with a ventral fin that had been removed in 1968—then that theory would not have held up. Also, there was the question of the crew. The Air Force flight crew would have had to have been part of the scam. There is no way any flight crew would have been fooled into thinking a forgery, just because it resembled their aircraft, was actually their plane. Every pilot, even if blindfolded, can tell his airplane by feel—much less a million other identifiers such as scratches in the paint and wear points on the control column, seat, throttle levers and virtually every other part in the cockpit. Tail number 26000, if the crew was not included in the conspiracy, had to be the actual Air Force One. What I had felt was a major breakthrough in the case seemed to be evaporating. I was disappointed that my specialized knowledge on this particular type of aircraft had not panned out the way I wanted it to—provided everything the Air Force historian said was true—but I wasn't defeated. Boeing Airplane Company never did reply to my letters, and there was still the matter of what happened *inside* Air Force One between Dallas and Washington.

The fact remained that the body could still have been taken out of the coffin, dropped down through the hatch, and then hidden in the aft baggage compartment for the duration of the flight. If this were true, just when could this have occurred?

It had to have happened in Dallas, before Air Force One left the tarmac. According to all sources, Kennedy's coffin was escorted by a loyal aide all the way to Andrews—except for one brief period.

Vice President Lyndon Baines Johnson decided that he just *had* to be sworn in as President *before* the jet could take off for Washington. Even against the Attorney General's and Jacqueline's wishes, LBJ made preparations for a swearing-in ceremony to take place *aboard* the aircraft, in the Stateroom, with everyone aboard present. He summoned a local Federal Judge to Love Field to perform the oath of office, and before the President's body was even cold, took the oath. A famous photograph shows him, right hand in the air and left poised flat on a *family bible*, looking solemnly at the judge while she spoke the words that would place him in the White House as President of the United States.

It was at this point that the body must have been removed from the coffin, dropped down the access opening into the aft baggage compartment, then sealed in a military-style metal shipping casket for the trip to Andrews. It was as simple as that. And with everyone not involved in the body transfer occupied forward, it was easy for two men to silently pop up from the lower compartment to fetch the body then disappear from view. Then it was a simple matter of riding to Washington in the baggage compartment. The casket guarded so faithfully during the flight by the Kennedy aide was empty.

This stage of the plan complete, it was now a matter of removing the metal shipping container from the airplane at Andrews and transporting it to where the physical evidence of the wounds—the direction of shot and the bullet fragments still in the brain—could be altered. The evidence of what happened at Andrews can offer an explanation on how this was accomplished.

As Air Force One taxied up to the ramp at Andrews, the media focused its attention on the aft passenger door on the left side of the aircraft. Within seconds of shutdown, a large gantry truck pulled up to that side of the airplane and raised slowly until it was even with the door. As all eyes watched, the bronze casket was carried out and placed on the floor of the gantry. Then, with the accompanying members standing around it, it was lowered to the ground.

With flashbulbs popping and movie cameras grinding away, the casket was carried the short distance to the gray Navy ambulance that would take it to Bethesda Naval Medical Center for autopsy. It should be noted at this time that Bethesda was *not* the original destination planned by the conspirators. Instead, they had made arrangements for the body to be altered at Walter Reed Army Hospital. But during the flight to Washington, an Army general told Jackie Kennedy that "We're all set. They'll be waiting for us at Walter Reed." But Jackie felt that her husband, since he was former Navy, should go to the Bethesda naval medical facility. An argument ensued, but the general, obviously outranked, gave in and returned to the radio compartment to make the new arrangements. Some time passed before he returned. Then when he did, he said words to the effect, "They're ready for us at Walter, er, Bethesda."

As the cameras locked on the casket being placed into the gray Navy ambulance, something else was happening on the other side of the airplane. A helicopter was warming up for take-off. As previously described, this is a definite violation of security procedures. But this helicopter had a purpose. It was to transport the metal shipping container and the two men in suits that crawled out of the aft baggage compartment doors on the right side of the aircraft to Walter Reed. For as the cameras and eyes of the crowd on the left side, which was bathed in camera floodlights, watched the proceedings, the opposite side of the aircraft was cloaked in darkness. The helicopter took off as soon as it was loaded and banked to the northeast—and Walter Reed.[39]

This particular incident had happened quickly. The helicopter hovered in within seconds after AF-1 came to a stop, landed to the right side of the fuselage behind the wings, then departed within two minutes. The event was even witnessed by newsmen standing on the left side of the aircraft, but the significance was not understood. One reporter described the arrival as, "...The President's jet is seen arriving, along with an *Army* helicopter."[40]

According to the historical chronology of the events, as stated in the book sent by the 89th Airlift Wing, here is what was recorded as the official documentation of the event. It bears inclusion at this point.

"...Following the assassination of the President in the early afternoon of 22 November (Friday), the body of John F. Kennedy arrived at Andrews at 1808 the same evening, accompanied by his widow; newly sworn-in President Lyndon B. Johnson, and his wife ladybird [sic]...The Air Terminal area was jammed with thousands of people, including the largest gathering of press and TV media ever assembled at anytime before in the history of Andrews Air Force Base. At plane-side, shortly *after the body of the slain President was removed to Walter Reed General Hospital*, President Johnson spoke briefly on the great loss of the 35th President of the United States."[41]

An Army medic working at Walter Reed remembered that night well. In one television documentary, he said that it was the first time in a long time that a helicopter landed on their helipad. As he watched, four men in suits got out and removed a long gray metal box from the aircraft and carried it into the morgue. A short while later they reappeared and re-loaded the box on the helicopter, which promptly took off and flew toward the northwest—the direction of Bethesda.

At Bethesda, other strange events were occurring. The gray Navy ambulance, whose driver had been forcibly replaced at plane-side by a Secret Service driver, had taken its time in getting to the hospital. In the interim, the helicopter from Walter Reed had arrived behind the hospital, off-loaded the shipping casket into a plain black ambulance or hearse, and departed. The shipping container was then driven to the back door, off-loaded by a party of six Naval Hospital Corpsmen, and rushed inside.

The NCO in charge of the off-loading detail was an E-6 named Dennis David. He had drawn the watch at the hospital as Chief of the Day. He not only supervised the off-loading of the plain metal shipping container at the morgue, but was told by Dr. Thornton Boswell, one of the physicians at the autopsy room, that Kennedy's body was in that particular casket. David, after leaving the autopsy room to return to the front of the hospital, was amazed that the gray Navy ambulance containing the ornate bronze coffin was parked in front of the main rotunda. He considered this highly suspect, as he could also see Jackie Kennedy and her entourage standing just inside the rotunda. If Kennedy was in the bronze coffin, then who was in the shipping container he had just watched being unloaded at the morgue?

Meanwhile, at the morgue, Hospital Corpsman Paul O'Connor began his duties by removing the body from the shipping container and placing it on the autopsy table. He described to Lifton that when the gray metal box was opened, the body was contained inside a rubber body bag. After removal from the body bag, the body was naked except for a bloody sheet wrapped around the head. As O'Connor prepared the body for the autopsy, he noted the head wound. "...The bullet...blew all of his brains out—literally. There wasn't anything to remove." When asked by Lifton, "What do you mean by that?" he responded, "The cranium was empty."

Yet a supplemental autopsy report was filed that described weighing "the brain." When asked where this brain came from, O'Connor said, "I don't know. That's another thing. I've heard about that too, and that's very puzzling because there was no brain in the body, near the body, or in the casket, or anything that I know of."[42]

By the time the autopsy began, an unusually large crowd had gathered in the autopsy room. The doctors who would perform the autopsy—none of which were experienced in traumatic gunshot wounds—were overwhelmed by the number of senior officers and civilian "suits" present. These senior officers allowed the autopsy to proceed, but whenever the doctors began to go into detailed dissection they were stopped. The pretext was that there was no reason to mutilate the body. The real reason was to make sure that no accurate finding was made of the wound analysis. For as expected, the body, after leaving Bethesda to lie in state at the White House prior to the funeral on Monday, was never viewed again. The services were "closed casket." There was no reason to not "mutilate" the body.

The head wound had been altered to such a degree that the direction of shot could not be determined. In fact, unlike the two relatively small wounds in the skull found at Parkland by Dr. Crenshaw *et al*, the skull now exhibited a huge hole that traversed the top right side from temple to rear.

There is a drastic discrepancy concerning this particular wound. If the brain had been blown out of the skull in Dealey Plaza, as was now indicated, then how did Kennedy manage to live for twenty minutes afterwards? According to Dr. Crenshaw, "Kennedy was barely breathing. The bullet that entered his neck had pierced the windpipe. Dr. Carrico had forced an endotracheal tube down his throat...When we saw blood frothing around the President's neck wound, it became clear that the endotracheal tube had failed to increase the air volume in his lungs. Dr. Perry [then] decided to perform a tracheostomy on the President's throat, where the bullet had entered the neck, between the second and third tracheal cartilages."[43]

The throat wound was another story. The Bethesda doctors could not even tell that a bullet hole was there, much less whether or not it was an entry wound. The original small tracheostomy described by Dr.

Crenshaw now gaped open as if someone had taken a meat cleaver to the President's neck.

But they did find something the Dallas doctors missed—the hole in Kennedy's back. In attempting to probe this wound, the doctors found they could only insert one small finger to the first joint. The hole was shallow—definitely not the through-and-through neck wound later credited by the Warren Commission as having passed through Kennedy to strike Connally. And before the doctors could begin dissection to determine if the path of the bullet changed direction internally, they were ordered to stop with that procedure and go on to the next. The autopsy was botched from the very beginning. Yet, the doctors cannot be held entirely to blame. They were career naval officers who were outranked by almost everyone in the room. And they had to either follow orders or risk losing their next promotion, or worse, their career—and their retirement pension.

Realizing the evidence supports the fact that Kennedy was struck in the back just before the head shot, it must be concluded, because of the range of the sniper positions behind the President that the bullet was fired from a rifle. But if it was, then why was the wound so shallow?

There are two circumstances in which such a wound could have occurred. First, the cartridge was defective. It was not uncommon for military surplus ammunition to misfire, either not detonating at all, or detonating with only enough force to push the bullet downrange at such a slow velocity that it would almost be harmless. Such a round might just make a slight hole, then fall out later relatively intact. Though this might have explained the "pristine bullet" found on the gurney at Parkland, it fails the test because it was found on a gurney in the hallway at Parkland that was not used by either Kennedy or Connally.

The second choice is a sabot round—a specially hand-loaded bullet—purposely fired to insert false evidence into the crime scene. In this case, either into the car or the body. It mattered not which, as long as "Oswald's" bullet could be found with enough rifling left intact to match the barrel of the 6.5 Carcano.

In 1975, a maintenance man named Morgan was working on the air conditioning system on the roof of the Dallas County Records Building, just south of the Dal-Tex building. While checking for water leaks, he found a .30-06 casing that had rolled back under some of the roofing tarpaper. Upon examining it, he found that it was weathered on one side only, bore the date-stamp '53, and the markings of the Twin Cities Arsenal.[44] It also had an unusual roll-type crimp around the neck of cartridge. This crimp is used to secure a plastic "sabot" liner on sub-caliber munitions. What that means is this: a 6.5mm bullet, with its relevant rifling left intact by being fired into a tank of water and recovered, can be reloaded into a larger casing, such as .30 caliber (which is 7.62 millimeter in diameter), and be used again. Only this time, the plastic sabot liner is what actually makes contact with the inside of the barrel, rides the lans and grooves, and picks up the rifling marks of this particular weapon. The bullet sheds the plastic liner, then travels downrange bearing the marks of the rifle from which it was originally fired. And if the round is undercharged, the bullet travels at much less of a velocity—with a reduced noise signature—until it comes to rest in the area intended by the shooter. In an opposite scenario, the sabot-type round is used to *increase* velocity and striking power. It does this by using the powder charge of a larger volume casing to propel a smaller, lighter bullet. In any case, it is evident that at some date and time a sabot round was fired from the roof of the Records Building, from behind the waist-high parapet that overlooks Dealey Plaza.

After the worst investigation in the history of American law enforcement, and a prompt coverup by the Johnson-appointed Warren Commission, the verdict given to the American public was simple: Lee Harvey Oswald, the lone nut with a cheap gun, shot the President of the United States. End of story.

But the Warren Commission itself was an exercise in disinformation and a travesty of justice. To begin with, all of the investigators picked to serve on the staff were lawyers. Not one experienced homicide investigator was called to serve. Therefore, the experience level of the staff to investigate a murder was nil. Then, of all the witnesses to the crime, only those who saw or heard something that reinforced the Commissions version of events—shots from the Book Depository only—were called to testify. Then, to make matters worse, LBJ gave the Commission a deadline in which to have the case solved—and closed.

Next, one must look at the members selected to serve on the Commission. Besides Earl Warren, there was John J. McCloy. McCloy was a high commissioner at the Nuremburg War Tribunal and was involved with coverups that ranged from the 26,000 American POWs liberated by the Red Army at the end of the war being kidnapped to Siberia and never returned, to Nazi scientists and technicians who were never tried for war crimes, but instead were smuggled out of Europe to the U.S. and Britain during Operation PAPERCLIP. McCloy also had been former president of the World Bank—with ties to several international financial and political interests.[45]

Then there was Gerald Ford. Ford was J. Edgar Hoover's private informant on the Commission. Whenever the staff investigators developed a new lead and began to get someplace, evidence under FBI control either disappeared, was altered, or fabricated as needed—prior to being requested by the Commission. FBI agents also intimidated witnesses, manipulated the language in reports and performed whatever machinations required by Hoover to cover the perpetrators.[46] In the case of Marina Oswald, for instance, 46 FBI "interviews" transpired during the two weeks following the assassination in which Marina was kept *incommunicado* by the Bureau. At the end of that time, Marina made several statements that would incriminate her husband, including claiming that she had taken the controversial photographs of Oswald holding the rifle and newspaper outside of their apartment. It is reasonable to assume that a Russian woman who wished to stay in American might say anything to preclude deportation back to the USSR.[47]

Allen Dulles was, for obvious reasons, an interesting selection. The former head of the CIA fired by Kennedy, whose brother was Secretary of State John Foster Dulles, could not have been a worse choice. It was a total conflict of interest to select someone in Dulles's position to investigate the murder of the man who cost him his career.

The three remaining members, Senators Richard Russell and John Sherman Cooper, and Congressman Hale Boggs, were harmless choices. They would neither help nor hinder the objective of the Commission. However, Boggs later became a problem when he began finding fault with the investigation. He refused to sign the final report, and not surprisingly, later ended up joining the long list of dead witnesses.

Over 177 witnesses have died in the intervening years since that bloody day in Dallas.[48] Of note are the following: Lee Harvey Oswald—killed by Jack Ruby; Jack Ruby—died of cancer (claimed he had been injected with cancer cells while in jail in Dallas); Roger Craig—reportedly committed suicide by shooting himself in the chest with a rifle (this was the fourth attempt on his life); Guy Bannister—died of a heart attack; Clay Shaw—died of a heart attack; David Ferrie—died of cancer.

Joining these were two of the three main Mafia players: Sam Giancana and Johnny Roselli. From the field action team both of the Grassy Knoll shooters were killed. Roscoe White was killed in a fire in Arkansas in 1975, and Lucien Sarti was killed in a shoot-out with police during a drug deal in Mexico City in 1978.

Alteration of evidence began on the day of the assassination and continued for years. First, the Carcano, examined in Dallas on the day of the killing, then flown to the FBI lab that night for another examination, failed to produce any fingerprints. But after being flown *back* to Dallas, miraculously showed Oswald's palm print on the barrel. This, after the rifle had been taken to the funeral home where Oswald's body was being held, for "comparison." The rifle itself was altered before it could be fired in the tests that followed. The sight was so loose and misaligned that it had to be shimmed and tightened before anyone could even fire the weapon with any degree of accuracy.

Kennedy's body, as mentioned, had been butchered. This was done for two reasons: to change the direction of the head shot, and to remove (by removing the brain) all particles of the exploding bullet fired by Sarti. The means were available in 1963 to match, by chemical and metallurgical analysis, bullet fragments. Therefore, every fragment in the brain had to be eliminated from possible discovery. The easiest, fastest and most effective way was to remove the entire brain.

The scene itself was sterilized. The curbstone where the stray bullet ricocheted to strike James Tague in the cheek was removed and replaced. The freeway sign, which had a bullet hole through it that came from the direction of the Grassy Knoll, quickly disappeared. The

Presidential limousine, which had a bullet hole in the windshield witnessed by two Dallas police officers, Sergeant Stavis Ellis and Patrolman H.R. Freeman, who saw it in the parking lot of the emergency room at Parkland, and by journalist Richard Dudman—made by a bullet fired from the front—was flown to Washington that night. It was taken to the White House garage where it was examined by a five-man FBI lab team that also noted the hole "just left of center" in the windshield. The windshield was removed and stored in the garage, but by the next week, the hole had disappeared—replaced by a nick now located on the *inside* of the glass. According to Ellis, it was not chipped glass at Parkland that he saw. "You could put a pencil through it." [49]

Case after case of altered evidence occurred. But over the years, other cases of new evidence began to appear. Perhaps the most startling were the assassination photographs, diary and three messages found by Roscoe White's son, Ricky.

Chapter 10

Messages To Mandarin

After his father's death in 1971, Ricky White went through Roscoe's possessions, one of which was a military foot locker. Inside he found photographs of the Kennedy assassination—and Lee Harvey Oswald—never seen before. He also found military records and photos and a diary written in his father's handwriting. He was shocked at what had been recorded. Among other things, according to the diary, Roscoe White admitted shooting President Kennedy. He also told an almost unbelievable story revolving around the assassination.

Ricky took the diary to the local FBI office. The agents there seemed mildly interested and conducted an interview with Ricky. But when the interview was over, Ricky took the material and returned home. It appeared that it meant little to the agents—perhaps they didn't believe him or didn't appreciate the value of the material.

But a short time after Ricky arrived home, one of the agents from the office showed up and explained that he thought his notebook got mixed up with the material when it was spread out on a table and might be in the box. Ricky showed him where the box of documents was and went into another room for a moment. When the agent left Ricky thought little about it. It was not until later, when Ricky began putting the items away, that he noted the diary was gone. This book, which contained a detailed account of the logistics involved in the operation and Roscoe's part, and it was never seen again.

The photographs were later taken in a burglary, but were eventually recovered in Arizona by the FBI and turned over to the Schweiker Committee, a subcommittee of the Senate Intelligence Committee. These photos were later made available to the Church Commission during their investigation of the murder and were never returned.[50]

About a year later, Ricky was in the attic of his grandmother's house when he discovered a metal artillery powder canister. The empty canister, ideal for sealing documents against moisture, contained several items of interest. Roscoe's Marine Corps service papers, his dog tags bearing the serial number 1666106, and three strange messages cryptically addressed to an individual—or an operation—codenamed "Mandarin."

The first message read as follows:

> CODE A MRC
> REMARK DATA
> NRC VRC NAC
> 1666106
> SEPT 63

Remarks - Mandarin : Code A :

FOREIGN AFFAIRS ASSIGNMENTS HAVE BEEN CANCELED. THE NEXT ASSIGNMENT IS TO ELIMINATE A NATIONAL SECURITY THREAT TO WORLD WIDE PEACE. DESTINATION WILL BE HOUSTON, AUSTIN OR DALLAS. CONTACTS ARE BEING ARRANGED NOW. ORDERS ARE SUBJECT TO CHANGE AT ANY TIME. REPLY BACK IF NOT UNDERSTOOD.

> C. Bowers
> OSHA

Re-rifle : Code AAA : destroy/ on/

The message was of standard format. It referenced an operation or individual codenamed "Mandarin," and the number in the top right hand corner was Roscoe White's Marine Corps serial number. At this time, Roscoe White was waiting to start the Dallas police academy. The ending reference, "Re-rifle," smacked of "Re: ZR/RIFLE."

The next message, addressed in similar fashion, was dated October, 1963. It also referenced "Mandarin."

DALLAS DESTINATION CHOSEN. YOUR PLACE HIDDEN WITHIN THE DEPARTMENT. CONTACTS ARE WITHIN THIS LETTER. CONTINUE AS PLANNED.

This message, as was the first, was "signed" by C. Bowers, OSHA, and referenced "rifle."

The third message was a bit worn. In one spot a word (or words) were missing. But in 1992 the words were finally made out and the subject was unmistakable.

STAY WITHIN DEPARTMENT WITNESSES HAVE EYES, EARS AND MOUTH. YOU [HAD NOTHING]* TO DO OF THE MIXUP. THE MAN WILL BE IN TO COVER ALL MISLEADING EVIDENCE SOON. STAY AS PLANNED WAIT FOR FURTHER ORDERS.

*Brackets indicate previously faded words.

This message was also signed C. Bowers.

As soon as Ricky White tried to make public the three messages, they were decried as a hoax by the investigative agencies of government. No motive for a hoax could be determined—after all who would want to go down in history as the son of one of the men who shot Kennedy—but they were nevertheless ignored by virtually every government official exposed to them.

But these facts ring true: Roscoe White was in Lee Harvey Oswald's platoon in Japan and later in the Philippines; Roscoe White worked in the intelligence community; he had access to a Dallas police uniform complete with badge; his serial number matched that of the message addressee number; and finally, the messages were of standard military format down to the last detail.[51]

Still, the fact remains that the investigative agencies of the U.S. Government have not followed up on either the diary or the messages to either prove or disprove their authenticity.

As the years passed and various forms of evidence surfaced, mostly due to the dogged determination of researchers and Warren Commission critics, other evidence was either being made unavailable or disappearing. The Warren Commission investigative files were sealed for 75 years by LBJ; the CIA files on Oswald and other players were either sealed, sterilized or removed; FBI agency files were either destroyed or found highly edited, and Hoover's private files—kept in locked filing cabinets in a secret room in his office—were destroyed *en total* upon his death; and the Dallas police files, opened in 1992, were found lacking in material substance regarding any form of conspiracy.

And files outside the "government" were also seized and/or destroyed. Of particular interest are the files which were removed by the FBI from Guy Bannister's office. These files, according to a list discovered by the Garrison team, included such titles as:

American Central Intelligence Agency
Ammunition and Arms
Anti-Soviet Underground
B-70 Manned Bomber
Civil Rights Program of J.F.K.
Dismantling of Ballistic Missile System
Dismantling of Defenses, U.S.
Fair Play for Cuba Committee
International Trade Mart
Italy, U.S. Bases Dismantled in
General Assembly of the United Nations
Latin America; and Missile Bases Dismantled—Turkey and Italy[52]

These are quite unusual files to be kept by a local private eye whose main business should have been snooping on divorce cases and investigating bogus insurance claims.[53]

THE KILL ZONE

The means of the coverup in 1963 were well-planned and well-executed. What is remarkable is not only the fact that it has remained intact for so many years, but that any effort made in exposing what really happened is still venomously opposed by not only those in power, but by the media. Even when President George Bush made a public announcement in 1992 (following a public outcry after the release of Oliver Stone's *JFK*) that he would open the long-sealed Warren Commission records, he changed his mind a few weeks later. There was no explanation and the records remain sealed. And as late as August, 1992, *U.S. News and World Report* published a feature article espousing the credibility and virtues of the Warren Commission.[54]

Someday all of the witnesses will be gone and the remaining physical evidence will disappear. At that time, the "files" will probably become available to the public. However, like the FBI and CIA files, they will have been "sterilized." The conspiracy and coverup will have succeeded and there will be no true and final solution to the murder.[55]

But a few questions will remain through the ages that will forever threaten to raise the demons of truth before the official version parroted by the government. The most obvious is the simple mechanics of the killing. Could Lee Harvey Oswald, given the 6.5mm Mannlicher-Carcano, fire a minimum of three shots accurately from the 6th floor window of the Book Depository in the time allotted?

This can now be answered. He could not.

According to my friend, Gunnery Sergeant Carlos Hathcock, the former senior instructor for the U.S. Marine Corps Sniper Instructor School at Quantico, Virginia, it could not be done as described by the FBI investigators. Gunny Hathcock, now retired, is the most famous American military sniper in history. In Vietnam he was credited with 93 confirmed kills—and a total of over 300 actual kills counting those unconfirmed. He now conducts police SWAT team sniper schools across the country. When I called him to ask if he had seen the Zapruder film, he chuckled and cut me off. "Let me tell you what we did at Quantico," he began. "We reconstructed the whole thing: the angle, the range, the moving target, the time limit, the obstacles, everything. I don't know how many times we tried it, but we couldn't duplicate what the Warren Commission said Oswald did. Now if *I* can't do it, how in the world could a guy who was a non-qual on the rifle range and later only qualified 'marksman' do it?"

The Marines were not the only ones who attempted to duplicate the shots. According to Victor Ostrovsky, an Israeli Mossad agent, the Mossad also tried to reenact the shooting using the available data. Using their best marksmen and finest equipment, they also found it couldn't be done by one man, using that position, in the time allowed:

> "To test their theory, they did a simulation exercise of the presidential cavalcade to see if expert marksmen with far better equipment than Oswald's could hit a moving target from the recorded distance of 88 yards. They couldn't...The Mossad had every film taken of the Dallas Assassination. Pictures of the area, the topography, aerial photographs, everything. Using mannequins, they duplicated the presidential cavalcade over and over again. Professionals will do a job in the same way. If I'm going to use a high powered rifle, there are very few places I'd work from, and ideally I'd want a place where I held the target for the longest possible time, where I could get closest to it, but still create the least disturbance. Based on that, we picked a few likely places, and we had more than one person doing the shooting from more than one angle....During the simulation, the Mossad, using better, more powerful equipment, would aim their rifles, which were set up on tripods, and when the moment came they'd say "bang" over the loudspeakers and a laser direction-finder would show where the people in the car would have been hit, and the bullet exits. It was just an exercise, but it showed that it was impossible to do what Oswald was supposed to have done."[56]

And to cap this, even the Soviets considered Oswald to be a poor shot. A Russian who knew Oswald in the Soviet Union told the TASS news agency that Oswald was a man "of weak character and poor marksmanship." The TASS article went on to say that Oswald at one

point bought a "hunting gun and joined a hunters' club. But he rarely attended training sessions and was considered a bad shot."[57]

And this simple fact—Oswald could not have done it—is the Achilles heal in the government's case. For the lack of planning and accomplishing two simple things—spending a few dollars more to buy a better rifle, equipped with an accurate sight, which was capable of the rate of fire alluded to, and finding a dupe that could shoot—a secret kingdom—the Entity—may someday fall.

Within two days of Kennedy's death, Johnson rescended the order to withdraw troops from Vietnam by signing National Security Action Memorandum No. 273—which had been written in draft form by William Bundy for LBJ's signature as President *on the 21st of November, the day before Kennedy's execution*—had moved into the White House, and had evicted Jacqueline Kennedy and her staff. JFK's famous wooden rocking chair was removed from the Oval Office—and the White House—on Monday, the very day of the funeral.[58]

Less than one month later, General Maxwell Taylor and Secretary of Defense Robert McNamara reported to Johnson that the situation in Vietnam was so grave that two things were immediately needed: American combat troops in great numbers, and a huge clandestine effort on the part of the intelligence community.

Those at the top tier of the organizational chart, their jobs secure now that "the king was dead," were now in position to profit financially. The *coup d' etat* had worked almost perfectly.

Almost. But the evidence that continues to surface proves otherwise. Fletcher Prouty sums it up: "It's one thing to kill somebody. It's another to hide the fact that you did it, or you hired someone to do it. And that's more difficult. That's why they used the device of the Warren Commission report to cover up their hired killers. Now who would hire the killers? And who had the power to put this report out over the top of the whole story? You see, you're dealing with a very high echelon of power. It doesn't necessarily reside in any government. It doesn't necessarily reside in any corporate institution. But it seems to reside in a blend of the two. Otherwise, how could you get the Chief Justice of the Supreme Court, the Dallas police, the media—all of the media, not just one or two newspapers—to participate in the coverup? None of the media will print the story, other than Oswald killed the President of the United States."

Other crimes and coverups committed by government organizations were to follow. But one chief question comes to light: *Are they connected*?

Are there hidden agendas that are held by certain powerful bureaucrats, politicians or secret groups that have remained intact through the years? Are the Machiavellian machinations of behind-the-scenes politics and power plays part of some sinister grand scheme? Do secret councils of power-masters meet behind closed doors in the halls of government and the high-rises of industry to plot activities outside of the law for their private benefit?

Or are the various conspiracies, crimes and their following coverups simply the result of certain influential individuals who have advantage of their political positions to line their own pockets and further their own careers?

In an attempt to answer these questions, and to understand many of the things that have happened since the Kennedy assassination, I found that it was necessary to investigate the historical events that led up to that fatal day in November, 1963. At first I traced events back to the very beginnings of America's participation in the war in Vietnam—back to the Eisehhower/Nixon administration of the Fifties. But I found a trail that led much farther back in time than that—farther back than I ever would have imagined. Though I found that it was during World War II that the major power structures learned how to create and use clandestine espionage services to further their own secret short-term political and financial goals, their overall long-term plan for the world—*The Agenda*—originated much further back in history than that. *Much* more.

The "simple homicide investigation" that began in Dealey Plaza had placed me on a trail that led into a maze of mirrors and mirages that would eventually expose me to a force more sinister, more powerful than the Mafia, the CIA, the Pentagon, Congress—even the White

House. When I entered the narrow door that led into the world of spooks and spies and Third World Wars, I began a journey that would take me to the summit of the highest mountain in the very depths of Hell.

And when I arrived there, I found what I felt to be the *real* reason John F. Kennedy was murdered.

Part II
Money, Murder and Madness

*And ye shall hear of wars and rumors of wars, See
that ye be not troubled, for all these things must come
to pass, but the end is not yet...for nation shall rise
against nation and kingdom against kingdom...but he
that shall endure unto the end, he shall be saved.*

Matthew 24:6-13

If you are going to fight a war and you intend to be the victor, you must have a clearly stated and totally understood military objective.

Carl von Clausewitz
On War

"Mr. President, you have told us to go over there and do 'it.' Would you care to define what 'it' is?"

Member of General Creighton
Abrams' staff, questioning
LBJ upon Abrams' assignment
to Vietnam.

"...The historical blame [for this defeat] must be placed squarely where it belongs...upon the very top civilian policy makers in Washington, specifically the Commander in Chief."

Hansen W. Baldwin
in Foreword to
Adm U.S.G. Sharp's book
Strategy of Defeat

Chapter 11

Chasing the Dragon's Tail

By the mid-1950s, former president Harry S. Truman had realized that the U.S. government's intelligence community—and particularly the CIA—was out of control. He often said that signing the National Security Act of 1947, which created the Central Intelligence Agency, was the biggest mistake of his presidency. Dwight D. Eisenhower, who was president at that time, had expressed similar sentiments. Both had discovered that the CIA had become a monster that lurked in the shadows, operated in secrecy, virtually without outside control and proper accountability, and had become a very dangerous animal indeed.[59]

Eisenhower was disturbed by a directive issued by the NSC that he perceived to be a vehicle that would give the CIA extreme powers and unlimited support for paramilitary operations. NSC directive 10/2, which was issued early in his first term, weakly defined the operational boundaries of both the CIA and the Pentagon. The NSC, who felt that the military's role in governmental affairs should be restricted to wartime only, and that the CIA should be responsible for peacetime covert activities, issued the directive that essentially ordered the CIA, whose resources at the time were limited, to turn to other agencies and departments for any needed support. On its face the directive appeared to recognize the CIA's lack of military hardware and logistical support, and would provide a vehicle to correct this shortcoming by allowing it to use the military's personnel and hardware upon request. It also was meant to send a message to the CIA that large scale military actions were the purview of the Defense Department and therefore would ensure that the CIA did not become some kind of separate army unto itself. Eisenhower, emphasizing this point, wrote in the margin of the first page: "At no time will the CIA be provided with more equipment, etc., than is absolutely necessary for the support of the operation directed and such support provided will always be limited to the requirements of that single operation."

Eisenhower then set up a watchdog committee to make sure all covert activities were monitored according to the directive, and to serve as a liaison between the CIA and the NSC and himself in regards to covert actions. The committee, serving as a subcommittee of the NSC, was created under NSC directive 5412/2. It therefore became the "5412 Committee," sometimes referred to as the "Special Group."

The 5412 Committee consisted of the Director of Central Intelligence (who acted as the operations officer), the President's special assistant for national security affairs, the Deputy Secretary of Defense, and the Deputy Undersecretary of State. By 1957, the Chairman of the Joint Chief's of Staff had joined the Committee. It was this committee, ultimately led by Vice President Richard Nixon, that would later be involved with the CIA's Executive Action program, the Laotian drugs-for-guns scheme, and the first covert aid and actions to South Vietnam.

NSC 10/2, after John F. Kennedy was elected, was twisted in meaning by the Pentagon. Instead of simply limiting the CIA's scope of operations and permitting the military to assist in a logistical manner, the military used it to conduct peacetime military operations—through the CIA. As Kennedy was assuming his office, a marriage was being performed between the Pentagon, the CIA, and the 5412 Committee.

According to *The Pentagon Papers*, "President Kennedy, who inherited a policy of 'limited risk gamble,' bequeathed to Johnson a broad commitment to war." This statement is totally false. Kennedy, as already shown, ordered troop withdrawals from Vietnam on October 11, 1963—six weeks before he was assassinated. The *New York Times*, in their publication of *The Pentagon Papers*, all but ignored the fact that Kennedy had signed National Security Memorandum 263 and had ordered the withdrawal to begin immediately, with 1,000 men to be pulled out within the following two months, and 1,000 more each month thereafter.[60] Also ignored is the fact that Lyndon Johnson effectively did away with NSM 263 with his own memo, NSM 273. This directive, signed the Monday after Kennedy's murder, canceled the withdrawal, committed America to support the Diem government in South Vietnam, and gave the president sweeping powers in dealing with the Southeast Asia situation. Incredibly, a draft copy of NSM 273, *prepared for LBJ* by William Bundy, was discovered in 1991 in the archives of the LBJ Library in Texas—dated November 21, 1963, *the day before Kennedy's assassination!*

Of the decisions made under this directive, one concerned the relatively small American force of helicopters that had been provided to Colonel Edward Lansdale's Saigon Military Mission by the Pentagon in 1960. This force, which consisted of a squadron of U.S. Marine helicopters, had been clandestinely transferred to Vietnam from its base at Udorn, Thailand in December 1960. The request for transfer of assets had originated with the Deputy Director of Central Intelligence, General C.P. Cabell, and had been made to the Office of Special Operations in the Office of the Secretary of Defense. Utilizing the authority granted under Eisenhower's NSC 10/2, the CIA operations in Vietnam began to escalate.

The helicopters that arrived in Vietnam were medium weight troop carrying Korean War-era Sikorsky H-19s. These would be followed eleven months later by a shipment of 33 Piasecki CH-21C twin-rotor heavy helicopters sent in from the U.S., along with sufficient pilots and ground crews to operate them. By November 1963, there would be more be more than 16,000 American soldiers in South Vietnam, most of which by then had participated in hundreds of ground combat operations and over 7,000 air sorties. The cost, which was hardly mentioned by the U.S. media, would by November 1963 include 23 aircraft lost to ground fire and 108 men killed in action.[61] It should be noted at this point that unknown to President Kennedy, secret dealings involving the CIA and the defense industry in relation to military support of Vietnam had been going on behind the scenes for quite some time. Shortly *before* Cabell made the request for helicopter support of the CIA Saigon Military Mission, the First National Bank of Boston arranged a special meeting with representatives of the Textron Corporation to discuss acquiring the then-foundering Bell Helicopter Company of Fort Worth. Bell, who had just completed initial design of the HU-1A medium utility helicopter, and who, by way of former Nazi general Walter Dornberger (rescued during Operation Paperclip), had lobbied the army to order 173 initial machines, was experiencing financial difficulties. The number of machines ordered would not be able to keep the company afloat for long, and even considering the possibility of replacing all medium helicopters in army inventory— Sikorsky H-19s and H-34s—the Cold War requirements would be satisfied within two to three years. It would take something more than a one-time re-equipment program to save the company.[62]

Yet the Textron Corporation, after a meeting in the Pentagon with the vice president of the Bank of Boston—a meeting that had been arranged by the CIA—decided to buy Bell Helicopter.[63]

Within a year, the HU-1A "Huey" had been redesignated the UH-1A and the first ships began rolling off the assembly line. Almost immediately orders were received from the Australian Army, and shortly thereafter from New Zealand, Indonesia, Norway and Columbia. To meet this amazing string of orders, a licensing agreement with Italy's Augusta helicopter company was issued by Bell.

The UH-1A, with its 770 shaft horsepower engine, was determined to be underpowered after a significant number were sold. It was updated to a new configuration with an improved rotor system, taller rotor mast, increased chord on the main blades, an aluminum honeycomb replacing the previous blade spar configuration, and a more powerful 960 shaft horsepower engine. This new variant became the UH-1B "Huey"—the uncontested workhorse of Vietnam.

By 1966, Bell/Textron UH-1s had replaced every U.S. Army medium helicopter in Vietnam, and had begun replacing the U.S. Marines' venerable Sikorsky H-34s. By 1968, almost every medium troop-carrying helicopter in Vietnam was built by Bell. This not being enough, the UH-1s took on the additional role of fire support. Both B and C models were equipped with weapons systems that ranged from six pylon-mounted M-60 machine guns (three to each side of the aircraft), to 7.62mm Gatling-style mini-guns, to rocket launchers that fired dozens of 2.75 inch high-explosive ballistic rockets. But these machines, though effective in providing firepower, were quickly determined to be extremely vulnerable to enemy ground fire. For this reason, the army decided in 1965 to put out bids for a dedicated attack helicopter that could serve the dual role of gunship and rocket ship.

The respondents were Boeing Vertol, who submitted an armed version of the huge CH-47 "Chinook;" Kaman, with their smaller UH-2; Sikorsky with the massive S-61, and finally Bell/Textron with the Model 209. The competition was short and sweet. By September of that year the first Model 209 had flown, and by April of 1966 the army had awarded a contract for two pre-production prototypes designated AH-1G Hueycobra. Only nine days later the army ordered 112 additional aircraft. The other four helicopter manufacturers had stood little chance in the competition. As a result, Boeing Vertol had to be satisfied with a limited production contract of 500 CH-46 and 270 CH-47 heavy transport helicopters, and Kaman had to settle for a production run of 198 HH-43B "Huskie" air force fire-fighting and rescue choppers. Sikorsky, by virtue of self-financing its research and development programs and earlier contracts with the navy and coast guard, was able to sell limited numbers of S-61 and HH-3 "Jolly Green Giant" rescue helicopters to the navy and air force. These few machines (120 in number) were eventually joined by the long-range HH-53 which inherited the Jolly Green Giant moniker from the aging HH-3s. Other than these examples, Bell/Textron produced the majority of the helicopters used in Vietnam. And, had there not been a glitch in another anticipated order, they could have produced more.

In 1961 a competition was held between Bell, Hiller Helicopter Co. and Hughes Aircraft to produce a light helicopter that could be used as a scout ship for ground forces. Bell was initially forecast by the

Pentagon to be the hands-down winner, and the "competition" was only a formality to satisfy the law concerning government purchases. But when the bids came in, Hughes beat the "prediction" and shocked the army procurement officers. Hughes priced their machines so low per-unit in anticipation of making their profits over the long term production of 4000 machines that the Pentagon was forced to award them the bid. However, in 1968, after producing only 1,417 OH-6A "Loaches" (for Light Observation Helicopter—LOH), the Hughes contract was cancelled and re-awarded to Bell who by then had developed the Model 206 JetRanger light helicopter. Designated OH-58, 2,200 "Kiowas" were purchased by the army and entered service in Vietnam. Hughes was conveniently and finally shoved out of future participation in the war effort.

In the end, Bell/Textron produced 7,387 helicopters for the Vietnam war.[64] Of all of the helicopters sent to Vietnam over 6,000 were shot down. Several hundred were transferred to the South Vietnamese army during Nixon's "Vietnamization," and all that left army inventory were replaced by the production of newer, more expensive units. Textron had done well to listen to the advice of the Boston bank. It was almost as if they had known something in advance.

The Bell/Bank of Boston/CIA/Pentagon/Textron affair is only one example of business conducted before, and during, the Vietnam war. There are more. For the companies who invested in the war the profits were enormous. Over $500 *billion dollars* were realized out of the war in Southeast Asia—almost all by a handful of private corporations.

To understand the gravity of what occurred, one must only look at who made and sold the war material vital to the military effort. At the beginning of major involvement by U.S. combat troops in Vietnam in 1965, the service rifle carried by all U.S. troops was the M-14, manufactured by numerous subcontractors. It was totally replaced within two years by the M-16, built solely by the New England firm of Colt Firearms. Five light and medium all-terrain vehicles were in service with the military that were built by five separate manufacturers—all replaced by a single vehicle, the M-151, built only by Secretary of Defense Robert S. McNamara's former employer, Ford Motor Company. And the list goes on.

But before any of this could take place, a *need* for such massive amounts of new, expensive equipment had to occur. Only involvement in a war could force such a need, and for this to happen, a change had to be made in previous U.S. policy decisions. Somehow, the U.S. had to be committed in force to the war in Vietnam, but that could not happen under NSM 263. Even if Kennedy's directive could be circumvented, the American Congress and people had to be incited. America had never been an aggressor, and no one would ever consider supporting the government in going to war unless we were provoked first.

The death of Kennedy permitted Johnson's issuance of NSM 273 which effectively negated the withdrawal of troops and committed American support to the South Vietnamese government. NSM 288, signed three months later, reaffirmed the commitment and explained in more definitive terms that America had to get personally involved to keep South Vietnam from falling to communism.

Getting more involved began thirty days later when OPLAN 34A was put into effect. A product of a JCS planning session in May 1963, OPLAN 34A called for covert operations against North Vietnam. These operations started with U-2 intelligence flights over the operational area of North Vietnam, followed by an escalating series of psychological and covert commando operations. Using specially procured high-speed patrol boats, CIA-trained raid teams were landed over the beaches of North Vietnam to sabotage various port facilities and defensive positions. As these operations were under way, C-123 cargo planes dropped other covert "hired personnel" beyond the North Vietnamese border to conduct similar operations—to include kidnapping and assassinations.[65]

Col. Fletcher Prouty, in his book *JFK: The CIA, Vietnam, and the plot to assassinate John F. Kennedy*, explains: "These 'hired personnel,' as a category of clandestine operators...are stateless people who are highly trained and equipped for special operations. They are far too valuable to expend on minor missions, and they must be kept available for such duties all over the world. They and their families are maintained in special safe areas, and their talents are called upon for covert operations of the greatest importance. The very fact that such key people were used in OPLAN 34A operations underscores how important the highest authorities considered these activities. "[66]

Still, to escalate the war, American troops had to be committed in numbers, and in such a fashion as to be supported by the American public. What Johnson needed was an incident.

Chapter 12

Manufacturing An Incident

On the night of August 4th, 1964, American television was interrupted by an emergency announcement made by the President of the United States. As alarmed Americans gathered around their TVs, the face of Lyndon Johnson appeared on the screen. His words, pronounced in a grave tone, carried a dire message to the American public. The U.S. Navy, while patrolling far offshore of North Vietnam in the Tonkin Gulf, had, without provocation, been attacked by the North Vietnamese navy. According to the President, this was the second attack. A previous attack had occurred two nights earlier, on August 2nd, when the U.S. destroyer *Maddox* was attacked by three North Vietnamese patrol boats which approached the warship 30 miles offshore and fired both torpedoes and surface guns. There had been no warning, there had been no provocation, and the *Maddox* was well into international waters. This was a clear act of war. Yet LBJ restrained from taking any counter-action on this incident. Instead, he responded that "The United States Government expects that North Vietnam will be under no misapprehension as to the grave consequences which would inevitably result from any further unprovoked military action against the United States forces."[67]

Then on the night of August 4th, according to Johnson, the North Vietnamese again sallied forth to take on the U.S. Navy. This time, an unknown number of small patrol boats—estimated by the relatively inexperienced radar man aboard the *Maddox* to be five in number—made their way through storm-tossed seas, on a moonless night, to attack not one, but two heavily armed U.S. warships that cruised 65 miles off shore. The *Maddox* on this night was accompanied by another destroyer, the U.S.S. *C. Turner Joy*. According to LBJ, this attack was "much fiercer than the first one," and had lasted almost three hours. Both destroyers returned fire and it was later reported that at least two of the attackers were sunk. President Johnson, who had issued his warning to the North Vietnamese government only two days before, now announced to the American people that even as he was giving his address to the nation, American fighter-bombers were winging their way toward the coast of North Vietnam to attack the naval bases from which the patrol boats operated. It was to be the first official retaliatory airstrike of the war.

It was this incident that led to the passage of the "Tonkin Gulf Resolution" by a landslide vote of 98 to 2 in the Senate and involved America in the longest war in the nation's history.

What really happened appears to be quite a bit different than the official version. On the night of August 2nd, South Vietnamese patrol boats—actually American-made Swift boats crewed by CIA-funded and trained crews—made an OPLAN 34A midnight commando raid on the Hon Nieu and Hon Me islands off the coast of North Vietnam. The North Vietnamese, in response to the attacks, sent out high-speed Soviet-built KOMAR class patrol boats. The KOMARs, instead of locating the escaping Swift boats, instead stumbled across the *Maddox* which was "providing support" in the vicinity. The government reports indicated that gunboats launched two torpedoes which missed the destroyer by 200 yards, forcing the *Maddox* to return fire with her five-inch guns. One patrol boat was reported disabled and the other damaged. Several aircraft dispatched to the scene from the U.S.S. *Ticonderoga* joined in and drove the attackers away.

The second attack, according to President Johnson, occurred on the 4th. On that night, contrary to LBJ's statements that the North Vietnamese were unprovoked, the CIA was again launching seaborne raids into North Vietnam. In this operation, the Vinh Sonh radar installation was attacked. This raid was followed by an "intercepted radio transmission" that supposedly stated North Vietnamese naval forces had been ordered to attack the patrol. This patrol, which consisted of the *Maddox* and *C. Turner Joy*, reported to be 65 miles off shore, was again assisted by naval aircraft to help repulse the gunboats.

One of the pilots that responded to the distress calls was Navy Commander James Stockdale. Stockdale, who later was shot down over North Vietnam and became a POW for over seven years, became a Medal of Honor recipient and eventually attained the rank of admiral. According to an article published in the October 1988 issue of *The New American*, Stockdale "found the destroyers sitting in the water firing at—nothing..Not one American out there ever saw a PT boat. There was absolutely no gunfire except our own, no PT boat wakes, not a candle light, let alone a burning ship. No one could have been there and not have been seen on such a black night."

Even the captain of the *Maddox*, John Herrick, radioed that official reports of the alleged enemy attack "appear very doubtful," and that there were no actual sightings by anyone aboard *Maddox*. It was later determined that what *Maddox*'s radar operator saw on the scope were probably wave caps created by the wake of the *C. Turner Joy*.

Even Daniel Ellsberg, who was working at the Pentagon at the time of the incident, said that "There was a great amount of uncertainty as to whether there was such an attack."

In regards to the first attack, which involved only the *Maddox* on the night of August 2nd, the ship was not in international waters as had been alluded to by Johnson. In fact, most sources now agree that the ship was somewhere between four and ten miles from shore and was supporting the OPLAN 34A CIA raid on Hon Nieu and Hon Me. This was verified by Saigon CIA Chief of Station John Stockwell who confirmed that the raiding boats had been working the coast all summer and were manned by CIA crews. Finally, regarding the U.S. government's claim that the North Vietnamese opened fire first, the log entries in the *Maddox*'s log state that the destroyer opened fire first—while the NVN KOMARs were still six miles away. By all indications and later interviews with crewmembers, it appears that the North Vietnamese, instead of opening fire with surface guns, actually turned tail and ran. There is now some discrepancy concerning whether or not the NVN boats even managed to fire the two torpedoes reported in the first version of the story. Considering the firepower of a U.S. destroyer, making a hasty retreat on the part of the NVN boat commanders upon recognition of the opponents would have been the sensible thing to do.

The Tonkin Gulf Incident, by all evidence that has surfaced since the dates in question, appears to have been orchestrated not from Hanoi, but from the White House. According to Jonathan Kwitney in *Endless Enemies: The Making of an Unfriendly World*, the "Tonkin Gulf Incident was a put-up job, designed to sucker the North Vietnamese into providing justification for a planned U.S. expansion of the war...The press was lied to, and so misinformed the public. We were all lied to."

To add weight to this is the recent discovery that the Tonkin Gulf Resolution—like NSM 273—was drafted by William Bundy, now Johnson's assistant secretary of state, *three months before the incident occurred!*[68]

The end result is that LBJ was given the power to increase U.S. troop involvement in Vietnam, and Eisenhower's infamous Military/Industrial complex was on another profitable adventure.

Chapter 13

Vietnam: The Enterprise

For General William Westmoreland, who commanded the Military Advisory Command Vietnam (MACV) during the early days of escalation, the objective was simple: body count. It was reasoned that the Vietcong could never withstand the mobility and massive firepower of the U.S. forces, and Hanoi's will to fight could quickly be broken by air power. But for the troops in the field, it was a matter of "search and destroy." Find the enemy, surround him with blocking forces, and annihilate him. Each such operation produced a body count, which offset enemy troop-strength estimates. MACV tabulated the progress of the war on visibly impressive charts with an elementary formula: the estimated enemy troop strength, minus the latest body count, left a number that supposedly constituted a substantially weakened force. The more bodies that could be counted, the closer the U.S. and South Vietnamese forces were to victory. The only problem was that the VC, and later the North Vietnamese Army conventional forces, were being increased in strength faster than they could be found and killed. And on top of this, body counts were often inflated to keep the brass in Saigon happy. This, unknown to the bean counters who reported to Washington, produced a totally false picture of the tactical situation.

The man who had the best understanding of how to deal with the war in Vietnam was a short, wiry, battle-hardened Marine Corps general named Victor H. Krulak. Lt. General Krulak served as special assistant for counterinsurgency and special activities on the Joint Chiefs of Staff in Washington during the Kennedy years. In 1964 Krulak left Johnson's Washington to serve as commanding general of the Fleet Marine Force, Pacific (FMFPAC) headquartered in Honolulu. This placed Krulak under Admiral Ulysses S. Grant Sharp, commander in chief, Pacific (CINCPAC). It was under Krulak that Operation Starlite,[69] the most effective operation in the entire war was conducted. Even though the command of the Marines fighting in Vietnam fell under the operational control (OPCON) of MACV—and General Westmoreland, and Westmoreland in turn answered to the Ambassador to Vietnam and the CIA Chief of Station in Saigon, Krulak authorized Starlite on his own responsibility and told no one until it was underway. Krulak knew that the worst chain of command in the history of American warfare existed in Vietnam and Washington. He knew that it was virtually ineffective.

But that's the way McNamara and LBJ wanted it. After all, the major decisions concerning the war were not made at MACV, or Honolulu, or even the Pentagon. They were made in the White House by LBJ and his civilian staff—not one of which had any combat experience.[70]

Krulak saw what was happening in Vietnam and determined that the situation was grossly mishandled. He later wrote: "I saw what was happening as wasteful of American lives, promising a series of protracted, strength-sapping battles with small likelihood of a successful outcome."[71]

To Krulak, this made no sense. Why were the politicians in Washington trying to run a military operation instead of giving the commanders a simple mission statement and letting them carry on with what they do best? Why had there not been a clear objective given the Pentagon? What was the plan?

Krulak, drawing upon his World War II combat experience, drew up a plan that would turn the war in Vietnam around and assure victory. There was nothing magic about it, it simply consisted of standard military tactics, procedure and technology that was available at the time to the theater of operations. It also took into consideration the problems inside the Vietnamese government and ARVN forces and suggested actions to correct them. Basically the plan consisted of three items: (1) Improve the South Vietnamese government and make it more responsive to the people; (2) Increase the training of South Vietnamese forces to make them more capable and combat ready than the opposing forces; and (3) Stop the flow of war materials to North Vietnam *before* they could be dispersed inland by mining the ports and harbors and destroying the docks at Haiphong.

Plan in hand, he flew to Saigon and met with Westmoreland. But for some reason, Westmoreland shied away from committing any forces to Krulak's plan. Undaunted, Krulak returned to Honolulu and presented his ideas to Admiral Sharp. Sharp liked what the Marine had to say and ordered him to catch a plane for Washington and show what he had worked up to General Wallace M. Greene, Commandant of the Marine Corps.

General Greene liked what he saw and made arrangements for Krulak to meet with the Secretary of Defense, Robert S. McNamara. McNamara, however, made no commitment. Instead, he passed Krulak on to someone who should have been entirely out of the loop—Assistant Secretary of State for Far Eastern Affairs, Averill Harriman. Harriman, who had previously served as Ambassador to the Soviet Union, invited Krulak to lunch and listened to what the general had to say. All seemed to be going well until Krulak got to the part where he recommended that U.S. forces "destroy the port areas, mine the ports, destroy the rail lines, destroy power, fuel, and heavy industry..."[72]

At that moment Harriman's face paled and he exploded "Do you want to go to war with the Soviet Union or the Chinese?" Krulak replied that he did not, and that it was unlikely that the Russians, or the Chinese—who the Vietnamese hated—would enter the war in Southeast Asia. Harriman did not agree and stated that mining the harbor in Haiphong would probably bring on hostilities with the Soviets. Krulak knew at that moment that if Harriman was advising Johnson on how to conduct the war, the troops in Vietnam were in trouble. Krulak, in his book *First To Fight*, wrote: "...our government failed to exhibit...courage and flexibility. As Governor Harriman made clear—and as our subsequent national conduct verified—we did not have the Washington-level courage to take the war directly to the North Vietnamese ports where every weapon, every bullet, truck, and gallon of fuel that was prevented from entering the country would ultimately contribute to the success of our arms and the preservation of our lives in South Vietnam."[73]

Krulak returned to Hawaii. He knew that he had to get the plan in front of the president, but the timing at the moment was obviously not good. He made another scouting trip to Vietnam in mid-1966 and, even more convinced that his plan would work and was necessary, returned to Washington immediately afterward. This time General Greene arranged a meeting with President Johnson in the Oval Office.

Johnson's first question was "What is it going to take to win?"

Krulak began outlining his plan step-by-step. He detailed the most important areas, pointing out the necessity of improving the quality of the South Vietnamese government and accelerating the training of the ARVN forces. But his main thrust concerned what he described as "...a self-defeating attritional cycle involving engagement with large and increasingly sophisticated North Vietnamese units." To break this cycle, Krulak brought out the logical answer: to stop the flow of war material to those forces.

Johnson asked if he were implying that the air campaign against the supply routes into South Vietnam and the staging and supply dump areas in the north were ineffective— considering that we were already flying 400-500 bombing sorties a day. General Krulak responded that for the most part the aerial armada was attacking the wrong targets. The "targets" designated by the White House consisted of "suspected" truck parks along the Ho Chi Minh Trail, secondary bridges, sampans, and empty jungle. The only effective measure that could be taken to cut off the supplies being delivered to the north would be to stop them before they crossed the docks. Once they entered the interior of the country and could be dispersed, or worse shuttled onto the Ho Chi Minh Trail complex, they were too hard to find in quantity and eliminate.

"I voiced the critical words," said Krulak, "urging that we 'mine the ports, destroy the Haiphong dock area...' that was it." That was a far as Krulak got. As soon as the general mentioned mining the harbors and destroying the Haiphong docks, Johnson stood up, put his arm on Krulak's shoulder and escorted him out of the room. That was the last time General Krulak, commanding officer of all Marines in the Pacific, ever saw the President.

Krulak was mystified. He could not believe that the Johnson inner circle would maintain a line of thinking that violated the very principles of warfare. As General Norman H. Schwarzkopf said of his tactics in Operation *Desert Storm* in a later period, "Amateurs think tactics, professionals think logistics." Johnson, however, had an aversion to completely cutting off the North Vietnamese ability to fight. "They were willing to spend $30 billion a year on the Vietnam enterprise," said Krulak, "but they were unwilling to accept the timeless philosophy of John Paul Jones [when he said] 'It seems to be a truth, inflexible and inexorable, that he who will not risk cannot win.'"[74]

Unknown to the Commander of FMFPAC, he had hit the nail on the head. Vietnam, to the inner circles in Washington, was not a war, it was an enterprise.[75]

Chapter 14

Help From The Strangest Places

There was a very good reason for not stopping the massive flow of supplies that was entering North Vietnam. For the upper level politicians and the defense contractors, the more war material that reached the North Vietnamese power base, the more that would be needed by allied forces in the south. One example of this occurred in early 1966 when the massive construction of U.S. facilities put such a strain on the U.S. steel-producing industry that the U.S. government had to go abroad in search of steel.

Miraculously, within days, several thousand tons of construction grade steel appeared on the docks of Singapore. The manufacturer of the steel could not be determined, as the identification markings had been removed prior to its arrival in Singapore from some mysterious outside source. This steel was purchased by the U.S. Government and shipped to Vietnam.

But someone inside the inner circle leaked some incredible information to the press. According to the December 18, 1966 edition of the *Washington Post*, "Peking Sold Steel to Americans for Viet Bases." Below this headline was the story that explained, "Communist China has sold several thousand tons of steel to Americans in South

Vietnam for use in the construction of new Air and Army bases needed in the growing war against the Vietcong...." The story went on to state, "The steel was sold through intermediaries in Singapore, who transshipped it to Saigon, and the Chinese Communists were paid through banks in Hong Kong." (Coincidentally, it appears that the identical transshipment ports—or "connections"were used for steel as were used for the opium coming out of Laos). The article ends with, "Reliable trading sources agree that all parties concerned, from Peking to the Pentagon, must have known both the origin and the destination of the bars."

What is incredible is that the same country that was supplying the North Vietnamese was selling cheap steel to their capitalist "enemy" that would aid in their war effort.

In that same year Dow Chemical Company, who made the infamous "Agent Orange" defoliant that was used in the jungles and Mekong Delta, experienced a shortage of magnesium. They, like the steel manufacturers, had to look overseas for a quick supply of the vital metal used in aircraft parts. As they were beginning the search a huge amount of magnesium appeared in Holland—a country that has no magnesium deposits. Within a few months Dow was in possession of several *million* pounds of magnesium.

Again, the *Washington Post* got the inside scoop. This time the headline ran, "U.S. Buying Magnesium from Russia." Without naming its source or a mysterious "American firm," the story explained "An American firm has bought a reported $2.3 million worth of magnesium—a metal vital in military aircraft production—from the Soviet Union in the past two months. Officials of the Dow Chemical Co. said demand for the magnesium has increased because of the Vietnam war." There was no doubt the U.S. government knew of the deal, for the article went on to say that "a 100% U.S. customs tariff charge required on shipments from Communist nations [had been applied]."

As a final example of dealings with strange commercial partners, there is the case of Camh Ranh Bay. At the beginning of the war, the equivalent of the Haiphong port complex in the south was initially Saigon. But the U.S. government felt that an additional port would be required to handle the massive infusion of military supplies expected to be needed over what was obviously going to be a long-term war.

Instead of utilizing the deep water port facilities at Da Nang, which already existed to a great degree and could have been easily and economically expanded, Johnson and his civilian "military advisors" selected Camh Ranh Bay, a shallow inlet only 150 miles north of Saigon. The bay, which offered little protection to large cargo ships, was too shallow to permit close-in unloading. Still, the White House was adamant about the bay area being developed.

One of the first orders of business, besides securing the area against Vietcong and NVA activity, would be to dredge the silt from the bay to increase its depth. For this, Johnson's long-time financial supporter, Brown & Root construction company of Texas, was issued the contract. The Vietnamese, who also wanted the work, were simply cast aside.[76]

It was about this time that the U.S. war effort received one of its strangest shipments of war supplies. With all of the construction going on in South Vietnam—Camh Ranh Bay, airfields, bases, highways (many of which being constructed by Brown & Root)—there was a sudden shortage of construction concrete. The U.S. suppliers could not keep up with the orders for cement, and once again the war-planners in the cabinet had to look abroad.

And once again, what was desperately needed—this time a huge quantity of bagged cement—was found in Singapore. Luckily for the U.S. contractors, the concrete discovered in Malaysia was cheap. That was because the heavy material, which was normally very expensive to ship, did not have to come from very far away.

Again the *Washington Post* had managed to get a scoop. In an article concerning the luck being experienced by the military in procuring war supplies, the *Post* stated that the cement *came from North Vietnam!* "The Haiphong cement was very cheap even though the cost of shipping it from North Vietnam was increased by special insurance payments against the risk of American air attack in the Gulf of Tonkin."

In the middle of the greatest bombing attacks since World War II, when North Vietnam was being reduced to rubble and would need every bit of domestic concrete available for its own use, the

115

communists were amazingly able to ship hundreds of thousands of tons of the precious mixture out of the country—at precisely the time the U.S. required it.

The companies that purchased these materials were in violation of U.S. law. The U.S. Battle Act specifically forbade U.S. companies from buying the majority of goods exported by communist countries. Even wigs which were made in Hong Kong had to be certified that they did not contain human hair taken from Red Chinese women.

But wigs were not critical to the war effort—or more specifically, to war profits.

Chapter 15

Operation Phoenix

As the triple-canopy jungles of Vietnam were being sprayed into oblivion by Agent Orange supplied in tonnage quantities by Dow Chemical, and millions of tons of war supplies were rolling across the beach at the Brown & Root-constructed Camh Ranh Bay to feed the growing American war machine, other, much more secret, affairs were taking place in the interior.

From the beginning, the Americans, who were used to dealing with enemies that wore uniforms and were therefore identifiable, were at a loss in dealing with the Vietcong who had no uniforms. In the words of Col. Fletcher Prouty, "...during wartime, the adversary, by tradition, is supposed to be in uniform. When the Yankee rebels at Lexington and Concord saw the redcoats coming, they had no trouble identifying the 'enemy.' Things were so different in Vietnam."

To deal with the army of pajama-clad guerrillas who, other than their ages and the fact that they carried AK-47s and grenades, resembled the civilian population, the military was forced to cordon off entire areas and then search them in detail to root out their hidden opponents. But these search-and-destroy—later to be referred to as "search-and-clear" missions— were only partly successful. They seldom turned up any leadership cadre above platoon or company level, and almost never produced any political infrastructure officers or high party members. To rectify this shortcoming, the CIA developed its own operation.

Codenamed Operation PHOENIX, this covert action program would be responsible for the death of at least 60,000 Vietnamese—many of which had nothing to do with the Vietcong whatsoever.

Largely carried out by special CIA-trained South Vietnamese operatives, the plan was initially conceived by the Agency. Its purpose was to identify, then capture or kidnap, or if necessary assassinate the members of the Vietcong command structure. According to former CIA director William Colby, who originally headed the CIA Far East Division and the Phoenix operations from 1968-73, "The CIA essentially initiated the process of trying to understand the secret communist apparatus in South Vietnam—we later called the Phoenix program—trying to gather together the bits and pieces of information: [such as] *who* is the local tax collector, *who* is the chairman of the district committee of the communist party and so forth...so that they become people and you can understand who they are. Then you can focus on trying to capture them, getting them to defect, or if necessary, shooting them."

This plan entailed working at night, inside the rural village complexes that provided haven for the VC. By using small infiltration teams of highly trained commandos, the CIA planned to remove key Vietcong from the villages, destroy the confidence of the VC in their ability to hide among the people, and eventually eliminate the guerrillas as a viable fighting force.

Robert Komer, President Johnson's personal representative in Vietnam, who held rank equivalent to the U.S. Ambassador, essentially ran the Phoenix program from 1967 to 1968. He recalled: "The CIA had been thinking about this program for years, and when I asked for suggestions on how we could get at the infrastructure, the CIA came up with the only ideas. State had none, and the military had none. And their intelligence on the VCI (Vietcong infrastructure) was, to put it crudely, zero!

"Frankly, I thought to devise a program to use the VC's own techniques to beat them. They were conducting a terror campaign, and I felt we should conduct a counter-terror campaign—to kill the VC assassins. And we did."

It sounded effective in theory. However in actual practice Phoenix, and its Vietnamese counterpart *Phung Hoang*, named after the "all seeing" bird of Vietnamese mythology, went astray. The Vietnamese intelligence agencies and province chiefs failed to fully participate. They each had their own agendas and political goals, and there was no such thing as an apolitical Vietnamese province chief or intelligence agency. For the Vietnamese, the war had two faces: fights with the Vietcong, and political infighting with each other.

Although President Thieu, at Komer's request, had ordered the intelligence agencies to cooperate, the military analysts at MACV noted, "The Phoenix-Phung Hoang program is looked upon by many Vietnamese as having been forced upon the GVN by the Americans." It was therefore resented as an unwanted intrusion into Vietnamese affairs. Another difficulty concerned the main objective of the program: identifying key officials and attempting to apprehend them in their homes. Many Vietnamese families had members in both the South Vietnamese forces, and the Vietcong. It was accepted in most instances by the Vietnamese that in normal circumstances such families were left unmolested by each side. It was one thing to kill a soldier in the field or a guerrilla during an ambush, and quite another to snatch either out of his native village when his brother or father was a member of the opposition. There was an attitude among the Vietnamese combatants that "if I don't bother his home, he won't bother mine."

To overcome this, Komer forced a quota system on the district and province chiefs. In this plan, a numerical quota was established that dictated how many VCI suspects had to be eliminated each month in order for the official to receive full Civil Operations and Revolutionary Development Support (CORDS) financial assistance for "economic development." In practice, the CORDS money became little more than bribes to produce a body count.

The CORDS program, set up in April 1967 under President Johnson and placed under Westmoreland's MACV command, provided the Americans with a way of centralizing the management structure for coordinating its many civilian and military aid programs. These specific programs were those used for "pacification" of the villages. To run the show, Komer was appointed by Johnson as deputy commander of MACV-CORDS. CORDS's budget for the next four years would exceed $1 billion per year.

Before CORDS assets were utilized and Phoenix formed, Komer had reported that pacification was like a business, and that "management of our pacification assets is not yet producing an acceptable rate of return for our heavy investment." When Phoenix and CORDS joined hands, Phoenix was put on a production quota basis similar to the numbers games played by the military and by the "Whiz Kids" of McNamara's staff in Washington. This strategy certainly did increase the output of the Vietnamese officials—in ratio to CORDS funding—but it also created problems. Alan Goodman, a scientist who studied the problems faced by the rural Vietnamese during the Phoenix program, wrote:

"During 1969, the primary problem faced by the rural population involved the injustices suffered under the administration of the 'Phoenix' program. Often, 'Vietcong' are arrested on the basis of anonymous denunciations received by the police from those who bear personal grudges against the 'suspect.' Of greater concern, however, are the large numbers of persons arrested in connection with the efforts of each provincial security agency to fulfill the quota assigned to it, regardless of the suspect's political affiliation, and it has not been unknown for province or police chiefs to seek each month to exceed their quotas in order to demonstrate competence."[77]

Congress got wind of the Phoenix program in 1971 and convened hearings on the issue. California congressman Pete McCloskey made a trip to Vietnam and examined the files on Phoenix targets to ascertain their credibility. In one he found that "...an individual was accused of being a potential VCI because while his village was occupied by the Vietcong, he had paid taxes to the Vietcong and his son had been drafted into the Vietcong forces. There was nothing to indicate that this man was engaged in making war against his own country." Little regard was given for the fact that most Vietnamese villagers cooperated with whoever occupied their hamlets at the time. They had little choice. Anyone who resisted or failed to provide support for the VC were executed.

Several witnesses were called before the hearings, many being former military intelligence officers. One such witness, Lieutenant Michael J. Uhl, who served as supervisor of the counterintelligence section of the 1st Military Intelligence Team (MIT), 11th Infantry Brigade, 23rd (Americal) Division, testified that there were basically two methods of determining who were VCI suspects. The first method that generated candidates was the search-and-destroy operations conducted by the Division. In these, scores of suspects—Vietnamese males of military age who were not in the ARVN—were rounded up and detained for interrogation. The MIT personnel then divided the suspects into two categories: "IC" for innocent civilian, and "CD" for civil defendants. According to Uhl, "There was an extraordinary degree of command pressure placed on the interrogation officer to classify detainees turned over to Interrogation [as] Prisoner of War [because] the way the brigade measured its productivity was not only by its body count and kill ratio, but by the number of CDs it had captured."

The second method of generating VCI suspects involved utilizing South Vietnamese informers and secret agents who provided lists of names that they indicated were Vietcong. The lists turned in at the Americal Division were then sent to the Phoenix teams for disposition. Uhl stated that there was no way for the Americal intelligence officers to verify the information on these lists. "We had no way of determining the background of these sources, nor their motivation for providing American units with information. No American in the team spoke or understood Vietnamese well enough to independently debrief any 'contact.' None of us were sufficiently sensitive to, nor knowledgeable of the law, the culture, the customs, the history, etc."

121

The motivation for the agents and informers to provide names was simple. Those that turned in lists were paid, those that didn't were not kept on the payroll.

Those suspects that were arrested were sent to the Province Interrogation Centers (PICs) for processing. At these centers the actual VCI were supposed to be weeded out from the innocent civilians. The weeding out process consisted of "psychological pressures." In plain language, torture. Some of the methods used included beatings; hanging a prisoner until he or she passed out then reviving them for another session; turning them upside down into a large vat of water and holding their head under until they almost drowned—then repeating the procedure, and other methods of physical and mental torture. One Vietcong suspect, a female who was a member of the education committee for the National Liberation Front (Vietcong) in Long An, reported after the war that she had been held in a PIC and tortured for hours. "When they tortured me," she recalled, "the Americans stood on one side and talked to my torturers. They used electric shock. First they attached a peg to my ear, then my lower lip, then my tongue, then my nipples. They had a device like a telephone set that had a gauge on it with markings from one to nine. When they turned it from one to eight, we were still conscious and felt pain. When they turned it to nine, we became unconscious. Then they hit my hands until they were all swollen like bananas and I couldn't close my fingers. Then they used a pair of pincers to pull my nails out, one nail at a time. I thought my fingers were going to drop off. When they pulled your nails, you felt a pain in the top of your head. It was terrible. It took ten years for my nails to grow back."

Reports of the outcome of the torture sessions were forwarded to the Provincial Security Councils for disposition. Here, each VCI, who may or may not have 'confessed,' was judged and sentenced.

Unless a bribe was paid. Alan Goodman reported that "With large numbers of helpless persons detained in province or district jails, opportunities for corruption have proliferated. In some provinces the Phoenix Program has been turned into a money-making scheme through which a villager's release can be obtained for payment of a bribe, usually about $25 to $50." The councils seldom cared if the suspect was guilty or innocent, as long as the money arrived to secure their release. Hundreds of actual VC were released in this way to fight again. Estimates in 1969 by the CIA concluded that by that time only about 30% of those arrested were retained at the provincial level.

To counter this, William Colby instituted a policy that required the Province Security Councils to sentence at least fifty percent of those prisoners turned over to them. During the congressional hearings, New York Congressman Ogden R. Reid asked Colby "How can you, as a concept, administratively, legally, or otherwise, set up a quota for what we might think are some kind of judicial proceedings? If you set a quota, is not that almost automatically saying we are setting a quota irrespective of the facts, the evidence or justice?"

Colby, avoiding a direct answer, replied that this was better than "filling the quotas by those who happened to be killed in the course of a battle." In this he was referring to the practice of identifying dead Vietcong on the battlefield as being high ranking cadre, adding their names to the Phoenix lists, then claiming them as a Phoenix kill.

According to Colby, the best use of Phoenix did not involve assassinations or battlefield kills, but instead live captures. Colby maintained that a live VC, who could be interrogated and might talk, was much more valuable than a dead guerrilla who merely became a statistic. It was because of this line of reasoning that Colby supposedly initiated the quota sentencing policy. At least there would be live prisoners to interrogate. It was to this end, Colby asserted, that Phoenix had originally been created.

But when asked by Congressman Reid if Colby could state categorically that Phoenix had never perpetrated the premeditated killing of a civilian in a non-combat situation, Colby answered, "No, I could not say never...individual members of it, subordinate people in it, may have done it. But as a program, it is not designed to do that."

Kenneth Osborne, a MACV-SOG intelligence officer who worked with the Provincial Reconnaissance Units (PRU) out of Da Nang under the cover assignment of a USAID refugee worker, recalled how it was in the field: "I never saw an official directive that said the PRUs will proceed to a village and murder the individual. However, It was implicit that when you got a name and wanted to deal effectively in neutralizing that individual, you didn't need to go through interrogation.

It was good enough to have him reported as a suspect and that justified neutralization. It became a sterile depersonalized murder program."[78]

Frank Snepp, a CIA officer who worked with Phoenix in the Tay Ninh province, was responsible for putting together lists of VCI that could be targeted for the Phoenix program. "It was an Alice in Wonderland war," related Snepp. "Nothing was as it seemed to be. I remember totaling up the number of kills that we had made through Phoenix operations, and I discovered that the number of kills far exceeded the shrinkage of the communist cadre apparatus. In other words, we were killing somebody, but they weren't communist cadre. The sin, from the American standpoint...was once realizing we were hitting the wrong people, we didn't stop. It degenerated into what amounted to an assassination program. I think it was the height of self-delusion for American officials to claim otherwise."[79]

According to Ralph McGehee, a CIA Vietnam vet who served in-country from 1968 to 1970, Colby not only knew exactly what was going on, he encouraged it. "The Agency was lying in one case, and all these murders were going on in another case. Colby, as head of CORDS, came up to province and sat there with his notebook and asked 'how many assassinations have we conducted? How many people have we arrested? How many firefights have we generated?' and I looked at him and said 'you dumb, blind son of a bitch! Why don't you open your eyes and see? Do you believe all these statistics you're reading? Do you believe all these things you're saying? How can you not comprehend reality?"

Colby admitted the war in Vietnam, as it was in Washington, was run on numbers. "We had quotas for absolutely everything. For numbers of guns to be handed out to the local population, for frequency of elections, we ran the war on numbers largely, and as a way of stimulating the local officers into paying attention to the matter—that was the way we stimulated them. Here we had an enemy that we estimated that was several tens of thousands, and so it was reasonable to say we'd like to see these people captured, or defect, or if necessary, killed."[80]

None of it worked. Robert Komer, who was sent back to Vietnam during the Nixon administration to assess the effectiveness of the Phoenix Program, found that "...the execution wasn't proving very effective. What we found was that most of the VCI that were being identified were villagers, which at best were at the lowest level of Vietcong infrastructure. Now we wanted to get Vietcong province chiefs, Vietcong tax collectors, Vietcong district chiefs, or the commander of the local defense battalion. We wanted to get the officers and then the men would all go home. We chartered the program on that. What we got were all privates—and missed the captains and colonels. "[81]

Colby eventually took credit for the 60,000 Vietnamese killed by the CIA's American, Korean, Filipino, Taiwanese and Vietnamese agents. At a cost of $4 billion, each Vietcong killed cost the U.S. taxpayers $66,666.00. (Quite a contrast to the $10,000.00 SGLI life insurance benefit paid to survivors of those killed in action, or the $11,125.00 paid to Agent Orange victims).

By 1975, Phoenix was over. The U.S. Army had already pulled out and the government of South Vietnam was collapsing. Nixon's program of Vietnamization had been a disaster, and the ARVN forces, riddled with corruption and poor leadership failed to hold the invading North Vietnamese Army back.

When the NVA reached Saigon, and the last American personnel were evacuated from the roof of the American Embassy by helicopter, thousands of documents were left behind in the three floors below—the offices of the CIA Saigon station. Of these, hundreds concerned the Phoenix program. The most damaging were not the damning reports of activities conducted by both American and South Vietnamese agents, but were the rosters of names and addresses of the agents themselves. No contingency plans had been made for *their* evacuation.

And they became the final victims of Phoenix.

Chapter 16

Moving Forward

By this stage in the investigation, I had learned that business dealings both at home an abroad had little to do with stopping Communism in Southeast Asia. Though the profit motive was very advantageous to the military/industrial/financial complex, there was some other game afoot. I found it incredible that a nation as strong in numbers and technology as the United States could not defeat a backward agrarian country such as Vietnam in a matter of weeks—much less years. Especially in retrospect. By this writing we have seen America's participation in three Third World wars: Korea, Vietnam, and Desert Shield/Storm. I could not help but note the ironic differences between the three.

First, the Korean War provided the first test of the United Nations' capability of fielding a multi-national fighting ("international police") force. The Korean campaign was the first war fought with "limited warfare" techniques and "rules of engagement" forced on the military by politicians—especially United Nations bureaucrats. The result was a stalemate, but the politicians were satisfied that their point had been made: the United Nations concept could work—at least in the eyes of the public.[82]

Second, Vietnam—which for some reason was *not* handled by the United Nations in a similar manner, even though the circumstances

126

were almost identical to those in Korea, resulted in a debacle of military mismanagement. The war in Vietnam appeared to show the American public, through the eyes of the media, that America—which had managed (in partnership with the British commonwealth) to defeat both Germany and Japan on a two front war in only four years just twenty years previous—could no longer fight a war without multi-national, multi-cultural assistance.

Third, Desert Shield/Storm, wherein the United Nations forces (98% of which just happened to be American troops and equipment) defeated a much more modern army than North Vietnam could field in a matter of weeks. Armed with near state-of-the art equipment, the Iraqi army died in less than two months under an onslaught that produced almost no casualties on the friendly side. It appeared to the American public that the only way to defend the U.S. in the future would be through the United Nations. After all, the war in Vietnam demonstrated that we were no longer capable of defending ourselves without outside help.

And that's exactly what the power-masters wanted.

Part III

Above The Law

Professing themselves to be wise, they became fools.

Romans 1:22

MONEY, MURDER AND MADNESS

"How can we account for our present situation unless we believe that men high in this government are concerting to deliver us to disaster? This must be the product of a great conspiracy, a conspiracy on a scale so immense that it dwarfs any previous venture in the history of man. A conspiracy of infamy so black that, when it is finally exposed, its principles shall be forever deserving of the maledictions of all honest men."

> Senator Joseph McCarthy
> 1951

"Your President is not a crook."

> President Richard Nixon
> 1973

"The charge has been made that the United States has shipped weapons to Iran as ransom payment for the release of American hostages in Lebanon, that the United States undercut its allies and secretly violated American policy against trafficking with terrorists. Those charges are utterly false."

> President Ronald Reagan
> 1986

Chapter 17

Coup *At The Watergate*

On June 17th, 1971, an off-duty police officer working security at the Watergate Hotel in Washington D.C., noticed something strange. While making his rounds on the floor where the offices of the Democratic National Convention (DNC) were located, he noted that one of the DNC's doors appeared to have had its lock tampered with. Upon closer inspection, he could see that the bolt had been taped—obviously to keep it from catching when the door was closed. He opened the door, peeked inside, but saw nothing unusual. At first he thought the maintenance people may have temporarily disabled the lock, but on second thought, knew that this was not the case because the tape was positioned along the edge of the door, not around the door in an obvious manner like he had seen in the past when hotel maintenance men had dealt with a faulty lock. He stripped the tape from the lock, checked the mechanism for operability, then closed the door, planning to come back later and check it again.

When he returned, he again found the lock taped. This time he backed off, called the police, and waited for backup. Within minutes an unmarked unit manned by two plainclothes officers arrived. After a quick briefing by the security guard, the three officers eased the door open.

They were presented with a startling scene. Five men wearing business suits, blue rubber gloves and carrying walkie-talkie radios, froze when they saw the officers guns. It was obvious to the police that they had interrupted a burglary, but one like they had never before encountered. For with the "burglars" was an impressive array of spy equipment: wire taps, cameras, and recorders. It was a most unusual encounter.

The events that followed would shake the nation's confidence in government to its very foundation, cost a president his job—and bring someone into the mainstream of government who had tried to achieve that level twice before, and failed. Someone who was already part of an organization much higher than the White House.

Early in the investigation it was determined that the five men caught inside the DNC were not common criminals. To the contrary, they were all members of, or were working for, President Richard M. Nixon's Committee to Re-elect the President—ironically dubbed "CREEP." Their identities, besides placing them in the ranks of CREEP, would also, to the knowledgeable political historian, provide a few additional clues—or doubts—concerning why they were in the Watergate.

First was the team leader James W. McCord. McCord was head of security for CREEP, but previous to taking this job, he had spent more than 20 years working for the CIA. By the time he retired from the CIA, he had become a high-ranking Agency security chief. Previous to his career with the Company, McCord had been a special agent for Hoover's FBI. To the astute observer, realizing McCord's experience and qualifications, it appears extremely odd that his team would have gotten caught. Especially considering the number of mistakes and poor tactical decisions they made during the fiasco.

Next in the rogues gallery was Bernard L. Barker. Barker was E. Howard Hunt's assistant in the months before the Bay of Pigs invasion, and had previously served as a Cuban secret policeman and double-agent under Castro. It was also Bernard Barker who was identified by Dallas police officer Seymour Weitzman, the first police officer to scale

131

the fence on the Grassy Knoll on the scene of the Kennedy assassination, as the man who showed both himself and Patrolman J.M. Smith credentials identifying him as a Secret Service agent.

Along with McCord and Barker, three other men were apprehended. Though the popular press reports of the time simply classified them as "Cuban Bay of Pigs" veterans, none had been on the invasion beach. Instead, as members of an elite team within Nixon's Operation 40, they had infiltrated into Cuba almost two months in advance with orders to assassinate Fidel. Each was a member of the ZR/RIFLE Executive Action assassination team.[83] These were Eugenio Rolando Martinez; Frank Sturgis (AKA Francisco Fiorini) who was recruiter and trainer for the ZR/RIFLE team under case officer E. Howard Hunt; and Virgilio R. Gonzales. Also of direct bearing was Felix Rodriguez (AKA Max Gomez) who was apprehended later as part of the operation. Rodriguez, who was responsible for tracking down and apprehending Che Guevara in Bolivia (after which Guevara was summarily executed), served as a CIA helicopter pilot in Vietnam during the PRU/Phoenix program, and later would be a key player in the Iran/Contra affair, serving as a supply officer at Illongapo Air Base in El Salvador under Oliver North.[84] [85]

The Watergate operation, as the ZR/RIFLE activity before it, was coordinated by former Operation 40 case officer E. Howard Hunt, who was now a White House aide and counsel for the financial arm of CREEP.

The five burglars, E. Howard Hunt and G. Gordon Liddy (also a White House aide and counsel for CREEP)—were later revealed to be part of a White House team known as "The Plumbers." Their job as such was to plug "press leaks" in the Nixon administration, of which there had been several.[86] Working under the direction and approval of John Mitchell—head of CREEP and former Nixon attorney general (and Nixon's former employer under Nelson Rockefeller during the early '60s)—the plumbers were given a new mission: infiltrate the Democratic National Headquarters, bug the telephones, photograph documents, and, from evidence that has surfaced since those dark days of 1971, possibly do a few more things that were not exposed until long after the investigation.

Of the public information that was presented during the hearings and investigations by the media, there were four objectives to be accomplished by the Plumbers. First, according to G. Gordon Liddy, the Plumbers were to bug DNC Chairman Lawrence O'Brien's telephone. The purpose of this wiretap was to find out exactly what kind of dirt the Democrats might have on Nixon that could be used against him in the coming election. Nixon reportedly was concerned with the prospect that the Democrats had managed to uncover certain shady land dealings he had with Howard Hughes and an under-the-table contribution by the billionaire recluse during his 1960 bid for the Presidency against JFK. During that campaign, a $205,000 "loan" to his brother, Donald Nixon, by Hughes Tool Company had been revealed and had a dire effect on Nixon's credibility. It has been reasoned that Nixon feared another such Hughes financial connection would have a negative impact on his bid for reelection, and it was therefore imperative to discover what the Democrats knew—and prepare to counter their expected attack.

Then, fearing that Hughes might be working both sides of the track, especially since it had been rumored that Hughes had secretly been paying O'Brien $15,000 a month to "represent his interests in Washington," and had secretly paid over $9 million to the Democratic Party to cover Hubert Humphrey's failed 1968 presidential campaign, it was imperative that Nixon get the details—and proof. According to Nixon biographer Stephen Ambrose, author of *Nixon: The Triumph of a Politician,* "For years, Nixon had been accused of being Howard Hughes's hired man in Washington. How sweet it would be to turn the tables and reveal that the chairman of the Democratic National Committee had been on a secret retainer for Hughes."

Next, information had come from the media that the DNC might be involved in running a Washington-based prostitution ring. On June 9th, eight days before the break-in, a front-page article ran in the *Washington Post* that stated that a prostitution ring had been uncovered by the FBI that was "headed by a Washington attorney and staffed by secretaries and office workers from Capital Hill and involved at least one White House secretary." Most damning among the evidence seized during the investigation were address books that named not only the hookers, but their clients. But it was not until it was discovered that Washington Attorney Philip Bailley was the man behind the hooker operation that the picture began to focus on the DNC. Supposedly unknown to the Democrats, Bailley was using the telephone number of R. Spencer Oliver, director of the Association of Democratic State Chairmen, to make contact directly to insiders within the DNC to arrange meetings between conventioneers and prostitutes. Oliver, who was normally on the road and away from the DNC offices, had no knowledge of the occurrences. According to Jim Hougan in his book *Secret Agenda: Watergate, Deep Throat, and the CIA,* a secretary in the DNC office would tell prospective clients to go into Oliver's unoccupied office and wait for the telephone to ring. They were advised that the phone would ring twice, and not to answer it. Then, when it rang again, they were to pick it up and make their arrangements. Once the customer had entered Oliver's office, the secretary made a call to another apartment in the building and told the answering party that a customer was ready to be contacted. Howard Hunt later stated that Oliver's telephone and office area was a primary target of the entry team.

If this was the case, there could have been a double objective to this particular target. Besides discovering the Democrats involvement in the ring to be used against them, it was also imperative that the Republicans perform damage control in their own house. It had been reported that there was a White House link, and if this was the case, the ammunition that could be used against the Democrats would be worthless. As it later turned out, a female attorney who worked in the Executive Office was involved in the ring.[87]

For whatever reasons, the team was selected and given their marching orders. They were to break in to the DNC, place eavesdropping equipment in strategic locations, photograph anything that might be of value, then get out without leaving a trace of evidence. It appeared to be a simple job for five men of such a talented background as the Plumbers, but everything that could go wrong did. In fact, so many things went wrong that it almost rings of sabotage.

First, McCord rented a hotel room across from the Watergate to serve as a lookout position for the break-in in the actual name of his private security company. Next, another room was rented in the name of Bernard Barker—one of the burglars. McCord then, for some obscure reason, tried to get approval from the Federal Communications Commission for the radio frequencies to be used by the entry team on their hand-held portable radios. This, according to G. Gordon Liddy, was akin to "registering a gun you're going to use in a holdup." Then, during the burglary, McCord ordered the team members to turn off their radios so that the static could not be heard from outside the room. This particular order came just as the security guard and police were beginning their search. Without radios, the lookout across the street could not warn the team of the danger and give them a chance to get away.

Finally, the act of taping the door lock doomed the men inside to discovery. McCord, attempting to be secretive by taping the lock vertically along the edge of the door only managed to draw the attention of the security guard as he made his rounds. These actions on the part of a seasoned CIA man are incomprehensible—unless he *wanted* to be caught.

But why?

Why would 53-year-old McCord, the $1,209-a-month chief security coordinator and electronics expert of the Committee for the Re-Election of the President, purposely sabotage the mission?

It is probably because McCord had never really left the Agency. There is no such thing as quitting—or completely retiring. As the saying goes, "Once a CIA man, always a CIA man." If McCord was contacted to perform a job for the Agency, it would be reasonable to assume that the job would be handled.

The question then arises: why would the CIA, or anyone else within the administration who could influence the performance of the Plumbers, want to force the mission to backfire? It would have to be someone, or some group, who wanted Nixon to be implicated, discredited—possibly even impeached. But who?

When one looks outside of the Watergate affair, to events that had taken place in the previous years of Nixon's political life, two major players surface that would have the motive and the means to effect just such a turn of events. The first is the military.

135

KILL ZONE

Top brass at the Pentagon had several reasons to axe Nixon. Among them were Nixon's handling of the war in Vietnam; his refusal to let the military planners participate in major foreign policy decisions; his blatant overtures to Red China—who was supplying the North Vietnamese with materials that were being used against American troops; his refusal to let American field forces in Vietnam prosecute the war as they saw fit; cutting the JCS out of negotiations with the North Vietnamese and instead putting the power in the hands of Henry Kissinger to end the war; and finally, the embarrassing fact that the Joint Chiefs of Staff had to infiltrate a mole—a Navy Yeoman named Charles Radford—into the White House as the aide-de-camp to General Alexander Haig, to steal documents from both Haig and Kissinger so that the JCS could stay abreast of what was going on behind closed doors.

The second entity that had the ability to influence the CIA, and a motive to derail Nixon, was one much more sinister—and more powerful than even the Pentagon. To recognize this entity and its motives, one must first answer two questions. These are: "Just who is Richard M. Nixon, and where exactly did he come from?"

In 1946, Richard Milhous Nixon, a 33 year-old naval reserve officer freshly back from World War II, was a small-town lawyer who had never held any political office.[88] Yet, six years later he was Vice President-elect of the United States. Only his running mate, Dwight D. Eisenhower, enjoyed such obvious meteoric success in the post-war years.

Nixon's public life began in 1947 when he ran for the California House of Representatives seat for the 12th District. In this race he faced Democrat Jerry Voorhis, a ten year veteran of Congress. Voorhis, who was an opponent of the New York banking establishment and the international banking cartel, and most importantly, an advocate for dissolving the Federal Reserve System, had made some very powerful enemies. During his time in office he had attempted to expose the monetary machinations between the Federal Reserve Board and the major New York City bankers and their European connections, and had even written a book, *Out of Debt, Out of Danger* detailing the organizations and the dangers they represented. For the money cartel, the threat of this pesky congressman had to be eliminated. The easiest way was to replace him with someone more sympathetic. Someone whom they could control.

With financial backing from members of the Council on Foreign Relations—a product of Rockefeller money from Standard Oil and the Chase Manhattan Bank, and Rothschild money from the House of Rothschild banks in Europe—Nixon defeated Voorhis and entered the House of Representatives in 1948. He was promptly appointed to the House Committee on un-American Activities, where he had a hand in exposing Alger Hiss as a KGB informant. This activity won the young Nixon the public reputation of being anti-Communist. Then in 1950, after a campaign filled with slander and accusations of being anti-American (and probably a Communist) against Congresswoman Helen Gahagan Douglas, "Tricky Dick," as he came to be known, slid into a seat in the Senate.

When Eisenhower was nominated to run for President against Taft and MacArthur in 1952, Nixon—who had ridden an anti-communist reputation since the Hiss affair—was selected as his running mate. He was only 39 years old. Within a time span of five years, Nixon had miraculously managed to serve in Congress, the Senate, and now was a candidate for the vice-presidency of the United States. Quite a remarkable achievement.

Eisenhower, it must be pointed out, had been similarly sainted by the money powers behind the government. A mere lieutenant colonel in 1941 (who had never seen combat), Eisenhower was promoted through the ranks of colonel, brigadier general, major general, lieutenant general, general, and finally general of the armies (five stars) by 1944. This was six complete major ranks in less than four years. No one else in the army was so fortunate.

Nixon's feat was even more remarkable in that he was not considered an Old Guard Republican. On the contrary, he was a left-leaning internationalist who had traveled to Europe with Christian Herter, a diplomat who had married into the Rockefeller oil empire, as a member of a committee that laid the groundwork for the Marshall Plan. Then, after joining Congress in 1947, he sponsored a resolution on the House floor that called for a "General Conference of the United

Nations pursuant to Article 109 for the purpose of making the United Nations capable of enacting, interpreting, and enforcing world law to prevent war." This was the same year the United Nations was formed in a meeting in San Francisco, wherein the U.S. delegation was headed by Nixon's later nemesis, *Alger Hiss*—who was picked to head the United States delegation by the Council on Foreign Relations!

Eisenhower's blast through the ranks of the military during the war was only a beginning to what would lay in store for him after the war. After commanding the U.S. occupation forces in Germany (where he had extensive dealings with John J. McCloy, who was the driving force behind forcibly returning the Russian POWs to Stalin during Operation Keelhaul, and who permitted Operation Paperclip to spirit away thousands of Nazis), he returned home to a much higher status level than when he left. Stephen Ambrose, an Eisenhower biographer, explained: "The elite of the Eastern Establishment moved in on him almost before he occupied his new office...[he and his wife] spent their evenings and vacation time with Eisenhower's new, wealthy friends. When they played bridge in the thirties, it was with other majors and their wives; in the forties, it was with the president of CBS, or the chairman of the board of U.S. Steel, *or the president of Standard Oil."* [Author's emphasis—Rockefeller family company] [89]

Eisenhower, whose education consisted mainly of his West Point military background, was made president of Columbia University in 1948. Coincidentally, in that same year he joined the Council on Foreign Relations—the front organization for the international banking cartel and international industrialists—and was appointed to the advisory board of the CFR magazine *Foreign Affairs.*[1] It was not a surprise when Eisenhower, through his CFR connections, was appointed supreme commander of NATO in 1950.

Most unusual about Eisenhower's past is that he had absolutely no party affiliation until 1952. In that year, at the direction of the CFR, he joined the GOP to run in the Republican primaries against Douglas

---

[1] The Council on Foreign Relations will be discussed in more detail in a later chapter.

MacArthur (who Truman had just fired from his command in Korea) and MacArthur's VP choice, Senator Robert Taft—the son of former president William Howard Taft, a pioneer anti-central bank and anti-Federal Reserve crusader. Strategically for the CFR, running Eisenhower against MacArthur was an excellent move: a general against a general—the commander of the armed forces in the Pacific against the commander of the armed forces in Europe. No one else would have stood a chance.

After selecting Eisenhower, the CFR bankers put their money and political apparatus into gear to get him elected. Even the media noticed what was happening behind the scenes. The January 23, 1952 issue of *Human Events* noted that pressure was being focused on key businessmen who "...favor Taft but have the misfortune to owe money to these Eastern bankers. We have, on investigation, spotted several cases in which businessmen...have received communications from their New York creditors, urging them to... raise or contribute funds thereto."

During the Republican National Convention, the cabal managed to have the Taft-favoring delegates from Texas, Louisiana and Georgia thrown out and replaced by Eisenhower people. One dirty trick followed another as the cards were re-shuffled and dealt. The end result was that Eisenhower and Nixon received the nomination. Taft explained that he and MacArthur had lost the race because of "...the power of the New York financial interests and a large number of businessmen subject to New York influence, who selected General Eisenhower as their candidate at least a year ago. Second, four-fifths of the influencial newspapers in the country were opposed to me continuously and vociferously and many turned themselves into progapanda sheets for my opponent."[90]

McGeorge Bundy, in an article in *Foreign Affairs* in October of 1952 stated that the nominations of Eisenhower on the Republican side and Adlai Stevenson (also a CFR member) on the Democratic side was not all luck. "These two nominations were not accidental...The fundamental meaning of the Eisenhower candidacy can best be understood by considering the nature of the forces he was drafted to stop—for fundamentally he was the stop-Taft candidate." The money powers had once again successfully controlled both sides of the ticket and produced a no-lose situation for the CFR.

Eisenhower, after winning the election, immediately moved to fill the offices of Washington with CFR members. For Secretary of State he approached his old friend and cohort from his German Occupation days, John J. McCloy. But McCloy reluctantly turned down the offer—he was busy holding the office of chairman of the Chase Manhattan Bank, and was about to take over as Chairman of the Council on Foreign Relations.

The job next fell to John Foster Dulles, brother of Allen Dulles and protege' of Woodrow Wilson, one of the driving forces behind implimentation of the Federal Reserve Act, in-law of the Rockefellers, and himself one of the charter members of the CFR. It is interesting to note that Dulles was also chairman of the Carnegie Endowment for International Peace and was the individual who had picked Alger Hiss for president of the organization. When Dulles died in 1959, Eisenhower replaced him with Christian Herter.

Dulles's brother, Allen, was picked to head the CIA. Allen Dulles, whose roots went back to the earliest days of the OSS and was instrumental in assisting Nazis to escape via the "Rat Lines," was responsible for the formation of the Cold War Gehlen Org spy network—and the salvation of SS General Reinhard Gehlen when Dulles was OSS Station Chief in Bern, Switzerland. Gehlen's bogus reports of Russian military strength forced Truman to order a massive military buildup to counter the supposed Soviet threat, and to increase the size of the 300-man Central Intelligence Group (CIG) to Agency status and strength (over 3000)—and that it was Gehlen's dormant Nazi spy network that accomplished the increase almost overnight. It was this conspiracy within the fledgling intelligence community that began the Cold War. Allen Dulles had been a member of the CFR since 1926 and later became its president. It should also be remembered that it was Allen Dulles who was fired by JFK after the Bay of Pigs debacle (which in itself should not be disregarded as a motivating factor leading toward his assassination).

Other CFR members picked by Eisenhower included: Robert Anderson for Secretary of the Treasury, Lewis Strauss for Secretary of Commerce, Douglas Dillon for Undersecretary of State for Economic

Affairs, Nelson Rockefeller for Undersecretary of Health, Education and Welfare, and Gordon Gray for National Security Advisor.

And Richard Milhous Nixon took his place as Vice-President of the United states.

Nixon, as vice-president, served two full terms. During this time he headed the CIA's infamous 5412 Committee (who oversaw Operations 40, Mongoose, Zapata and the ZR/RIFLE team) rubbed shoulders with the New York City banking community, the president of Pepsi Cola, officials of ITT, the Howard Hughes organization, and even a few questionable characters who had links to organized crime. By 1960, He had become the Republican Party's candidate for the Presidency opposing John F. Kennedy.

At this same time, New York Governor Nelson Aldrich Rockefeller also sought the Republican presidential nomination. But he could not win the grass roots support outside of New England necessary to secure the nomination and had to temporarily resign himself to being the power behind the throne.

Theodore White, in his book *The Making of the President, 1960*, explained that Nixon was summoned to Rockefeller's private New York apartment to discuss the GOP platform: "A single night's meeting of the two men in a millionaire's triplex apartment in Babylon-by-the-Hudson, eight hundred and thirty miles away [from the Republican Convention], was about to overrule them [the Republican National Committee]..." The end result of this clandestine meeting was that Nixon would answer to the major New York bankers—and Rockefeller. For this, there would be substantial support for his campaign. Edith Kermit Roosevelt, writing about the Nixon/Rockefeller meld, commented: "It was not as a Standard Oil heir, but as an Establishment heir...that Nelson Rockefeller forced the Republicans to rewrite their platform. Thus the Republican platform was in effect a carbon copy of the Democratic platform drawn up by Chester Bowles, CFR member and former trustee of the Rockefeller Foundation."

It now becomes apparent that the big-money East Coast cartel had control of both parties (though unknown to them at the time, not necessarily both candidates), and Nixon's surprise defeat in the election (a result of Mafia kingpin Sam Giancana's rigging of the ballot boxes in Illinois, and LBJ's similar actions in Texas in favor of Kennedy) was of no major concern. Kennedy assumed the office of President—and Nixon joined the Council on Foreign Relations.

The following year, during the California gubernatorial election, conservative candidate Joe Shell told Nelson Rockefeller that he would not support him in his bid for the Presidency in 1964. One week later, fellow CFR member Richard Nixon, who until that time had shown no interest in the position, announced his candidacy for governor. Nixon failed to unseat incumbent Democrat Edmund G. "Pat" Brown, but did succeed in defeating Shell in the primary—which was good enough for Rockefeller.

Nixon returned to New York, where he joined the law firm of John Mitchell—Nelson Rockefeller's personal attorney. His residence in New York was located at 810 Fifth Avenue, which just happened to be the same apartment he and Rockefeller had met in during the 1960 campaign. Rockefeller, who owned the building, by that time had moved to another apartment in the same building. Needless to say, over the next eight years Nixon's personal wealth increased substantially while he was Rockefeller's tenant, employee, attorney, and neighbor—even though he did relatively little law practice.

In 1968, Rockefeller again made a try for the Presidency. This was his third attempt, and again he failed to rally enough support to put his name on the ticket as a contender.

Nixon, however, did manage to secure the support necessary to run. No one seemed to notice his odd pro-Communist (and globalist) leanings at the time, even though he had written a very enlightening article only a few months previous for *Foreign Affairs* magazine, the periodical of the CFR. Titled "Asia After Vietnam," he mentioned that new inroads could—and should—be made in relations with Red China. Relations with Communist China had been a long-time goal of the CFR and Nixon, under Rockefeller's guidance, would later see that this goal became a reality. In the article he wrote of the need "to evolve regional approaches to development needs and *to the evolution of a new world order*." [Author's emphasis][91]

This was exactly what Nelson Rockefeller and the CFR wanted. A new world order—controlled by the CFR and the international banking cartel.

Nixon, with the backing of the CFR, defeated Democratic contender Hubert Humphrey in the 1968 election—and the timing could not have been worse for a new president to enter office. The war in Vietnam was at its highest point; race riots and peace demonstrations rocked the country; the drug scene was totally out of control (LSD and heroin usage, due to the CIA's Operation MK/ULTRA and the government's importation of CIA-supplied Laotian heroin being at an all time high); law enforcement was faced with a soaring crime rate; and the national debt was climbing by the minute. The only way Nixon could fight such numerous and massive brush fires was to enlist the aid of capable people—who had the right connections—to administrate the government. Like Eisenhower before him, he turned to his old benefactor, the Council on Foreign Relations. By 1969, the CFR had provided Nixon with 110 of its members—the greatest number appointed by any previous president.

The most important appointee provided by the CFR was Henry Kissinger. During John F. Kennedy's term, CFR member McGeorge Bundy, a Harvard professor who taught a class called "The United States in World Affairs," was picked by the Council to serve as National Security Advisor. He in turn was "advised" by Kissinger, who succeeded him at Harvard when he entered government service. Then, when Nixon needed to fill the position, Kissinger, who had by then authored several articles for *Foreign Affairs* concerning the war in Vietnam and how to conduct peace negotiations with the North Vietnamese, appeared. It comes as no surprise that Kissinger, who also served as Nelson Rockefeller's chief advisor on foreign affairs, would be Nixon's choice to serve as the key negotiator with the North Vietnamese in Paris.[92]

Problems continued to build for Nixon, Rockefeller, and the CFR throughout 1970-72. Expose's of the Wall Street-White House connection such as Gary Allen's *None Dare Call It Conspiracy*, and former FBI agent W. Cleon Skousen's *The Naked Capitalist* were published and began shedding light on who actually controlled the government. But the money powers, who controlled the major media, managed to conduct adequate damage control. Allen's book, which sold over five million copies, was not even mentioned in any major newspaper or any of the three television networks.[93] Then, as a diversionary tactic, articles appeared in the *New York Times*, and in *New York* magazine that gave the impression to the public that the CFR was little more than a club filled with foreign policy dinosaurs that had no connection with, or influence over, the Nixon administration. The articles failed to mention the number of CFR members appointed by Nixon to key government positions.

Nixon twice offered David Rockefeller, Nelson Rockefeller's brother and president of the Chase Manhatten Bank after John McCloy in 1960, the position of Secretary of the Treasury. But David Rockefeller considered even the presidency a step down from his then-current position as Chairman of the CFR and on both occasions turned him down. Other key members of the CFR did accept key posts offered by Nixon. Peter G. Peterson, who would replace David Rockefeller as Council Chairman in 1985, would become Secretary of Commerce. Arthur Burns became Chairman of the Federal Reserve Board (a critical position for the world bankers), and Charles Yost became Ambassador to the UN. Other important positions filled by CFR members included:

Elliot Richardson: Secretary of Health Education and Welfare.
James Lynn: Housing Secretary.
George Ball: Foreign Policy Consultant.
Dr. Paul McCracken: Chief Economic Aide.
Harlan Cleveland: Ambassador to NATO.
Jacob Beam: Ambassador to the USSR.
Gerard Smith: Director of the Arms Control and Disarmament Agency.
George H. W. Bush: UN ambassador after Yost.
Casper W. Weinberger: chairman of the Federal Trade
    Commission.

Other appointees, such as George Shultz (Treasury secretary), Melvin Laird (Secretary of Defense), and David Kennedy (Treasury secretary), joined the CFR after appointment to their respective positions. Another interesting "Nixon" choice was Texas Governor John Connally, who succeeded David Kennedy as secretary of the Treasury. This selection of a Democrat gave mute testimony to the fact that outside influences superseded party politics when it came to naming players. There was little doubt exactly who controlled the government.

By 1970, the professed anti-Communist Nixon had turned into a traditional liberal. He had failed to reduce Lyndon Johnson's 435 welfare programs, and was actually in the process of expanding them; he raised foreign aid; proposed the Family Assistance Plan (FAP) which guaranteed an annual income to every family (a federal handout financed by taxpayers); and made major overtures to the governments of both Communist China and the Soviet Union. Syndicated columnist James Reston wrote:

"It is true that Nixon rose to power as an anti-Communist, a hawk on Vietnam, and an opponent of the New Deal, but once he assumed the responsibilities of the presidency, he began moving toward peace in Vietnam, coexistence with the Communist world of Moscow and Peking, and despite all his political reservations, even toward advocacy of the welfare state at home." [94]

He added in 1971:

"The Nixon budget is so complex, so unlike the Nixon of the past, so un-Republican that it defies rational analysis... The Nixon budget is more planned, has more welfare in it, and has a bigger predicted deficit than any other budget in this century." [95]

Richard Nixon, the world began to see, had become a socialist. The off-shoot of his surprisingly liberal activities, however, were of great benefit to certain capitalists: those that loaned money to the government—the banks of New York and Europe.

145

The Rockefeller and Rothschild banks.

Nixon was re-elected for a second term and the debt to the bankers continued to increase. The war in Vietnam, which had dragged on for over ten years, continued to consume millions of dollars in material each day, and Kissinger seemed to be no closer to a peaceful solution with the North Vietnamese than ever. Disentangling from Vietnam appeared to be more difficult than Nixon had promised during his campaign when he outlined a plan of "Vietnamization" wherein the South Vietnamese would take over from the Americans and, with the continued infusion of American equipment and financial backing, finish the conflict on their own.

When Kissinger finally did manage to work out a means of withdrawal from Vietnam that would give Nixon his rhetorical "peace with honor" solution, it was an extremely one-sided affair. The agreement would allow the North Vietnamese to keep all of their troops (almost 300,000) in place in South Vietnam, force the U.S. to remove all military units, and promised Hanoi war reparation funding to rebuild their bombed-out country. It should be remembered that the pawns in this last promise were the only bargaining chips the North Vietnamese held: the POWs.

The details of Kissinger's agreement with Le Duc Tho did not seem to effect the average American. After being continuously bombarded by the media with negative reporting of the war for years, and watching helplessly as the casualty list grew, most cared little about *how* the country got out of Vietnam, but only that it did so.

It was Nixon's promise of peace that influenced his reelection, and it was the Peace Accords agreed to by Kissinger that won Kissinger the Nobel Prize. Yet the end result was the loss of South Vietnam, Laos and Cambodia—and a genocide of millions of Asians that followed. And the debt for the war remained to plague subsequent administrations *ad infinitum*.

By the time Watergate occurred, the national debt to the international bankers was at an all time high, Vietnam's usefulness as a profit generating vehicle had ended, the government employed more CFR members than ever before, and Nixon's usefulness as president had virtually come to a close.

Watergate was the vehicle that put Nelson Rockefeller into the administration—almost into the the White House itself.[96] For when Nixon's house of cards began to fall, a strange series of events transpired: Vice-President Spiro Agnew was forced to resign after being advised that he was under investigation for taking kickbacks from private contractors when he was a Baltimore County executive (1962-66), governor of Maryland (1967-68) and even vice-president; Nixon was forced to resign or face impeachment proceedings; Gerald Ford, who had served as J. Edgar Hoover's inside man on the Warren Commission and who steadfastly maintained Oswald's guilt to the exclusion of all others, was ironically selected to replace Nixon; Ford then pardoned Nixon for all crimes and coverups he had been involved in and gave him immunity to prosecution—then selected Nelson A. Rockefeller as his Vice-President.

There is one more area of interest concerning the Watergate break in. It concerns the 18 1/2 minutes of tape recordings that were erased from the Oval Office tapes that were eventually surrendered under great protest to Judge Sirica's court. It has been speculated that the conversation that took place during those missing minutes concerned the Kennedy assassination. Especially since other references on the tapes showed that Nixon was, for some reason, very concerned about "that Bay of Pigs thing."[97] By 1974, the Bay of Pigs debacle was ancient history. What could possibly surface at that late date that would be any more embarrassing to anyone in government than already had? Unless the terminology was a reference to something else, such as the ambush in Dealey Plaza.

On August 5th, 1974, Nixon finally released three tapes to the public which revealed that he had been in on the coverup from the very beginning. This information, along with the July 30th House Judiciary Committee's recommendation that Nixon be impeached for charges of obstruction of justice, abuse of presidential powers, and trying to impede the impeachment process by defying committee subpoenas, caused Nixon to resign from the Presidency four days later on August 9th.

On September 8th, 1974, Gerald Ford granted Nixon a "full, free and absolute pardon...for all offenses against the United States which he...has committed or may have committed or taken part in during the period from January 20, 1969, through August 9, 1974."

The time frame designated by Ford's pardon covered Nixon's entire term of office.

By the end of 1974 the banking cartel had cleared another hurdle in American history. Nixon was out, Rockefeller (and Ford) were in; the CFR had infiltrated more players into government than ever before in history; the national debt to the banking cartel was at an all-time high; and the American public, war weary and exhausted by the media blitz, had become numb to the happenings in Washington. The power brokers behind the throne had never been in a more advantageous position.

Chapter 18

The Chairman: A Man Of Many Talents

Winston Churchill called it "The High Cabal." Colonel L. Fletcher Prouty, JFK's Director of Covert Operations for the Joint Chiefs of Staff, called it "The Power Elite." Others knew it as "The Enterprise," "The Council," "The Committee," and other names. But no matter what it was called, the organization that has pulled the political strings of government since before World War I in not only the U.S., but Europe, Russia and Japan, exists. It is resident in four major areas of international affairs: the international banking community; certain, selected boardrooms of major corporations; cells within the command structure of the military services of the most powerful of countries; and within the secret corridors of the covert intelligence community. It is an all-powerful organization that makes its own laws as needed, disregarding any that happen to be objectionable, utilizes the covert intelligence services of virtually every major country as footsoldiers during peacetime, and their military machines in times of war.

Such an elite and powerful organization requires highly educated, extremely qualified, and very loyal individuals to fill its upper echelon ranks. The astute student of history will note that during the past eighty years, many of the same names appear over and over within the administrations of the upper levels of government. Often these names are not in the forefront of historical events, but certainly involved in a staff or advisorship position. It is these people who truly control the fate of the nation—and the other nations of the world. And it is these people who are consistently awarded key positions and promotions, and continue to serve within the hallowed halls of government from one administration to the next without fear of replacement. It is this resiliency and continued success in ascension that, even though they attempt to hide behind other, more visible figures, identifies them for what they are: members of The Power.

One shining example of such a person was John J. McCloy.

Throughout the pages of this work Mr. McCloy's name has surfaced over and over again. From his days of presiding over the SWNCC during World War II to serving as President Kennedy's counsel for Nuclear Disarmament, John J. McCloy personifies the character of those picked to represent the Power. To understand just how influential and powerful the Entity really is, one only has to examine the career profile of its agents.

They say that you can tell a lot about a man by who attends his funeral. If this axiom holds true, John Jay McCloy—affectinately known as "The Chairman" to his friends—was indeed an important man. Though his name only appeared as a bit player in many major political scenes, it would appear that he was much more than that by the scene that unfolded on the day of his funeral.

Inside the Brick Presbyterian Church on Manhattan's fashionable Upper East Side, gentlemen wearing expensive custom-tailored coats and suits crowded into the pews that faced the alter. Those who might recognise these men would find an elite gathering indeed. There were lawyers from the most prestigious Wall Street law firms: Milbank, Tweed, Hadley & McCloy; Cravath, Swaine & Moore; and Cadwalader, Wichersham & Taft. There were representatives of AT&T, Dreyfus, Squibb, Allied Chemical Company, Westinghouse, Metropolitan Life Insurance Company, Mercedes Benz, and virtually every major American oil company. And then there were the investment bankers of Kuhn, Loeb, and the commercial bankers of Chase Manhattan Bank.

There were representatives from the Ford Foundation, the Rockefeller Foundation, the American Council on Germany, the Aspen Institute, and the Atlantic Institute. Members of the New York Bar Association, the Bond Club, the Century Club, and other fraternaties were also apparent, and most of all, had someone had a roster, it could have been noted that most in attendance were members of the Council on Foreign Relations—including Richard M. Nixon who sat in the front pew with former chancellor of Germany Helmut Schmidt and James A. Baker, the new secretary of state for President George Bush.

Serving as ushers were: former chairman of the Federal Reserve Board Paul A. Volcker; Kennedy national security advisor McGeorge Bundy; Texas oil billionaire Perry Richardson Bass; Carter secretary of state Cyrus R. Vance; Ford Foundation officer Shepard Stone; former chairman of Lehman Brothers Peter G. Peterson; and Richard M. Furland, chairman of Squibb Corporation.

Giving eulogies were: Alexander Forger, lead partner of the law firm of Milbank, Tweed; former West German President Karl Carstens; former Chancellor Helmut Schmidt; Secretary of State Baker; former Secretary of State Henry Kissinger; David Rockefeller; and John J. McCloy II.

It was indeed a powerful showing.

John Jay McCloy was born in Philadelphia on March 31, 1895. The son of an upper middle class father who worked as auditor for Penn Mutual Life Insurance, he became the man of the house at an early age when his father died. To provide for the young John's education, his mother, Anna May McCloy, went to work. John attended the Peddie School in Highstown, New Jersey, where he began to develop the athletic skill which made him the captain of the tennis team at Amherst College.

After obtaining his B.A degree *cum laude* from Amherst in 1916, he enrolled at Harvard University to study law under Professor Felix Frankfurter (later of the Warren Court). But with the entrance of the United States into World War I, the twenty-two year-old McCloy in May of 1917 interrupted his studies to enter the army. After initial training at Camp Plattsburg, New York, McCloy was commissioned a second lieutenant and assigned to the 19th Cavalry at Fort Ethan Allen, Vermont. Within weeks the cavalry regiment was reorganized into the 77th Field Artillery under the 4th Division and was ordered to Europe. From this moment on, McCloy would, like certain other prodigies before and after him, find himself hitched to a rapidly rising star.

After arriving in France with the AEF, McCloy was transferred to the 160th Field Artillery of the Second Army. Here, he became operations officer and was rapidly promoted through 1st lieutenant to captain. With the Second Army, McCloy served between the Moselle River and Verdun. When the Armistice came he was selected for more responsibility and transferred to Advance General Headquarters at Treves. From there he was assigned to serve with the German Occupation forces of the Third Army at Koblenz in Germany—an assignment that would be of great value later.

McCloy resigned his commission in 1919 and returned to Harvard, where he reentered law school and graduated LLB in 1921. Upon graduation he miraculously was offered a job with the prestigious Wall Street law firm of Cadwalader, Wickersham and Taft. He worked for this firm for the next four years, then moved to the firm of Cravath, de Gersdorff, Swaine and Wood—to become a full partner in 1929. It was during this time that he worked on the infamous "Black Tom" espionage case of 1916 involving a massive bombing of a munitions plant on Black Tom Island in New York. For three years he traveled in Europe, and served as the firm's representative in Paris. In 1939 he successfully presented the Black Tom case, which the insurance company had refused to pay citing "arson" as the cause, to the Mixed Claims Commission at The Hague. McCloy provided evidence that it was an act of German sabotage, which convinced the Commission, and the case was finally settled.

The following year, Secretary of War Henry L. Stimson appointed McCloy, who at that time was described as "having a flourishing law practice, practicing corporate law,"[98]on Wall Street, to "Expert Consultant in Espionage." This may have been in reaction to the Black Tom case, but for whatever reason from this point on McCloy began to accumulate power and influence faster than almost any other human being. Thirty days after this appointment he was promoted to Special

Assistant to the Secretary of War (Stimson), then only four months later, in April 1940, was appointed Assistant Secretary of War.

Europe was by now aflame with the first actions of World War II. Germany had invaded Poland and the Sudetenland, France was about to undergo the *Blitzkrieg*, and British forces were massing what they could of their British Expeditionary Force to help the French contain Hitler. Meanwhile, the Japanese were posturing for a military contest in Asia and the Pacific. It was in this atmosphere that John J. McCloy re-entered government service.

To provide the clearest view of McCloy's career for the next 25 years, and to be as concise as possible, a simple list of achievements must suffice. The reader will find it alarming.

As Assistant Secretary of War, McCloy:

1. Secured Congressional passage of the Lend Lease Act.
2. Fostered the special intelligence unit that broke the Japanese Code.
3. Supervised the internment of Japanese Americans on the West Coast.
4. Advocated the formation of the *Nisei* units of Japanese Americans in the U.S. Army for combat duty in Europe.
5. Helped form the French Committee of the National Liberation in North Africa.
6. Prevented the shelling of the German town of Rothenberg (the ancestral home of the Rothschild family).
7. Presided over the SWNCC (State, War, Navy Coordinating Committee) who ultimately was responsible for choosing what targets in Germany would—or would not—be bombed; tracking down and hiding Nazi scientists under Operation PAPERCLIP; deciding which Nazi war criminals would be tried at Nuremburg; and making the final decisions regarding the handling of POWs and MIAs in Europe.
8. Advocated civilian control over the Pentagon and in making major military decisions over those of Pentagon/military planners.
9. Participated in the formation of the policies toward liberated areas—which would be of great value later when he entered the civilian banking world.

10. Helped prepare armistice and surrender terms for Germany and Japan.
11. Supervised the administration of occupied territories and became chairman of the Civil Affairs Committee.
12. Attended conferences at: Casablanca, Potsdam, Cairo, the United Nations conference in San Francisco—but mysteriously never was shown in photographs of the times at these locations.
13. Was a major player in formulating the plans for the Nuremberg Trials, and was instrumental in deciding which Nazis would (and would not) be tried.
14. Was one of the few civilians in upper government circles who was privileged to know of the Atomic Bomb and the intention to use it against Japan—and exactly which cities were targeted.
15. Recommended, along with OSS officers Allen Dulles and Frank Wisner, former SS General Reinhard Gehlen to serve as the eyes and ears of the Western intelligence community in Eastern Europe—even though he had been designated a war criminal.

In November, 1945, McCloy resigned as Assistant Secretary of War and returned to private practice with Milbank, Tweed, Hope, Hadley and McCloy in New York City. That shift to civilian life did not last long. Within a few months he succeeded Eugene Meyer as president of the International Bank for Reconstruction and Development. The IBRD, or World Bank as it became known, was a specializing agency within the newly-formed United Nations used to lend money to war-torn nations—such as Germany and Japan—for reconstruction. It should be remembered at this point that only a few months before McCloy had been integral in selecting enemy targets for non-destruction (which meant conversely that other cities were then automatically selected *for* destruction). During McCloy's one-year tenure as president of the World Bank, over $8 billion dollars were loaned and profits of $650 million were achieved for the New York banks who provided the funds.

In 1946, McCloy became a member of the Department of State Committee on Atomic Energy. Then in June of 1949, President Harry Truman appointed him High Commissioner of Germany (HICOG) and military governor of the American Zone of Germany. This made him the ranking official of the Economic Cooperation Administration within the country, and also made him a key figure in rebuilding German businesses and banks. During his three years as HICOG, McCloy granted West Germany over $1 billion in economic aid—all from the World Bank and certain New York banks that he would have further dealings with later. At the same time, he was instrumental in forcing the early release of many ex-Nazi war criminals (who did not escape under Operation Paperclip during the initial transfers) and getting them jobs in private industry both inside Germany and abroad.

In 1952, McCloy returned home to become a consultant to the Rockefeller-financed Ford Foundation, which is closely aligned with the Council of Foreign Relations on domestic and educational matters. The following year he became the Chairman of the Chase National Bank, which dealt with thousands of banks and businesses around the world—especially the Rothschild banks of Europe. Within twenty-four months, the Chase Bank merged with the Bank of Manhattan to become the Chase Manhattan Bank—the second largest bank in the world after the Rothschilds. At the same time, he served as Eisenhower's unofficial advisor for disarmament negotiations.

McCloy remained with Chase Manhattan until December 1960, when he "retired" to return to private law practice with Milbank, Tweed, Hope, Hadley and McCloy. Again, his private law practice lasted a very short time. One month later he was designated by the newly-elected John F. Kennedy as his principal disarmament advisor and negotiator. This followed on the heels of his unofficial service under Eisenhower, which made McCloy, a Republican, one of the few carryovers from the previous administration. This job lasted until October 8th, 1961, when he resigned after an altercation with the President over Kennedy's decision to resume nuclear testing.

It may seem that wishing for nuclear disarmament was the sign of a man of peace, but to the powers above the White House, there was a more personal reason to be concerned over nuclear weapons. To them, the discovery and employment of the atomic bomb was a mistake. Even though they provided the funding and resources required for the research and development of the bomb at Oak Ridge and Los Alamos, it was not until after the war that the simplicity of construction made the bomb a significant problem for the cabal. Simply put, the bomb was a threat. It theoretically could take power away from the superpowers and give it to anyone with the capability of scientific research. This, as in today's case of Iraq, Iran, and possibly Libya, shifted the balance of power to those who could not be controlled by such entities as the CFR or its European counterpart, the Royal Institute of International Affairs. In a nutshell, the all-powerful would not be quite so powerful if someone not under their direct control had such weapons. Therefore, if a private agenda were to be adherred to, such weapons would have to be neutralized or taken away by disarmament.

President Kennedy, after learning of Kruschev's resumption of nuclear testing, made the decision to do the same. McCloy resigned in protest.

John J. McCloy disappeared from public view until December 1963—when he was appointed as a Commissioner on the Warren Commission to investigate the assassination of John Fitzgerald Kennedy.

McCloy did not disappear after the Warren Commission, but did maintain a much lower public profile. Between 1964 and his death in 1989 he was involved with numerous dealings between the U.S. government and other governments; private industry and the banks; private industry and the government; and the bankers and the Federal Reserve Board. His name was also seen in dealings that range from SALT talks to the MIRV, and from domestic oil companies to OPEC. He wore so many hats that on one occasion Senator Clifford Case wondered aloud how McCloy could have "represented everybody, including the U.S. government without the U.S. government knowing what was being done until [McCloy] told them about it."[99]

By the time of his death, McCloy's law office had accumulated some very impressive memorabilia. On its walls hung the autographed photographs of such personalities as: General John J. "Black Jack" Pershing, General George C. Marshall, General Lucius Clay, General George S. Patton, General Omar Bradley, Konrad Adenauer, James Forrestal, Lyndon B. Johnson, John F. Kennedy, Gerald Ford, Dean Rusk, Henry Kissinger, and of course his mentor, Henry L. Stimson. Richard Nixon's likeness also hung there, in what McCloy called his

"Rogue's Gallery," but took the form of a trophy. It was not autographed.[100]

Eisenhower, who went from lieutenant colonel to five-star general in less than 40 months, and Nixon who rose from small town lawyer to Vice-President of the United States in five years, both passed through the court of the CFR and its representatives—men like John McCloy. Each in turn received the graces of the botherhood, and each stood briefly in the spotlight of fame and fortune until their usefulness was over. But McCloy, and others like him, continued to maintain their respective positions behind the throne as presidents came and went. And whenever possible, they stood well out of the circle of light.[101]

But not out of the circle of power.

Part IV

Sinister Purpose

For we wrestle not against flesh and blood, but against principalities, against powers, against the rulers of darkness of this world, against spiritual wickedness in high places.

Ephesians 6:12

ABOVE THE LAW

I suggest a radical alternative scheme for the next century: the creation of a common currency for all the industrial democracies, with a common monetary policy and a joint Bank of issue to determine that monetary policy.

Richard N. Cooper
Article in *Foreign Affairs*
Fall, 1984

We shall have a world government whether or not you like it, by conquest or by consent.

James Warburg
Testimony to Senate sub-committee,
February 17, 1950.

You may say I'm a dreamer, but I'm not the only one. I hope someday you'll join us, and the world will be as one.

John Lennon
Imagine

Chapter 19

The Plan Exposed

By following the twisted trail that led from Dealey Plaza to the highest circles of power, I discovered that the greatest conspiracy in American history was not the assassination of John Fitzgerald Kennedy. Instead, I stumbled across a plot so criminal in nature and intent, so diabolical and sinister, that it defies belief. It is a centuries-old conspiracy that is being conducted by the powers that reside well above our government. It rests not in the hallowed halls of Congress or within the Oval Office, but instead where power really lies: the closed societies of the mega-rich and the private boardrooms of the super-banks.

It has been said that money is power. This is true. But when history is examined it can be determined that the majority of the world's monetary assets fall into the hands of a few privileged families and the banks and businesses they control. The names of these families are no secret; they are the social elite of Europe and America that have controlled the destiny of nations for over two hundred years. Only by understanding where world power really emanates can we understand exactly *who* makes up the power behind the throne of not only the United States, but every modern country in the world today.

SINISTER PURPOSE

*   *   *

It all began in a little goldsmith's shop in Frankfurt, Germany, in 1773. The proprietor of the shop, 30 year-old Mayer Amschel Bauer, had an obsession: he wanted power and wealth. In actual fact, he wanted much more than that—he wanted to rule the world! To anyone else, this was a ridiculous dream. But to Bauer, it was an attainable goal if one had the proper plan of action and the resources to finance it. The obstacle that stood in his way concerned his lack of personal resources, and projected income, which prohibited him from implementing his plan of action within his lifetime. If he were to try for the gold ring, he would have to have help.

In that year, Bauer invited twelve wealthy acquaintances to a meeting at his shop. The purpose of the meeting was to convince them to pool their fortunes to finance a world revolutionary movement—which they would control—with the ultimate purpose of gaining the wealth, natural resources, and control over the population of the entire civilized world. After the guests had gathered he explained the purpose of the meeting and quickly outlined his ideas: by combining their wealth, and cleverly manipulating it in the form of loans to sovereign governments until the governments were well within their debts, they could create crises and economic conditions that would range from prosperity to unemployment, peace to war, which would in turn force the governments to borrow more money—which would put them even more into debt to the conspirators. Bauer summed up his feelings concerning the true base of power when he said: "Permit me to control the money of a nation, and I care not who makes the laws."[102]

When the twelve conspirators agreed to pool their resources, Bauer presented his plan and its ideology in detail:

1. Paid propagandists will arouse feelings of hatred and revenge against the ruling classes by exposing real and alleged cases of extravagance, licentious conduct, injustice, oppression and persecution. *They will also discredit anyone who might discover, and subsequently interfere with, our goals.*

161

2. The first principle to remember is that Law is Force in disguise. By the laws of nature, right lies in force.

3. Political freedom is an idea, not a fact. *In order to usurp political power all that is necessary is to preach "Liberalism"* so that the electorate, for the sake of an idea, will yield some of its power and prerogatives into our hands.

4. The power of gold usurps the power of Liberal rulers. It is immaterial to the success of our plan whether the established governments are destroyed by external or internal foes, because the victor has to, of necessity, ask for capital which is entirely in our hands.

5. The use of any and all means to reach our final goal is justified on the grounds that the ruler who governs by moral code is not an effective politician. His morality demonstrates weakness and leaves him in a vulnerable position.

6. Our right lies in force. The word "right" is an abstract thought and proves nothing. "Right" means to attack by the Right of the Strong, to reconstruct all existing institutions, and to become the sovereign lord of all those who leaves to the enterprise the rights to their powers by laying them down in their liberalism.

7. *The power of our resources must remain invisible until the very moment when our movement has gained such strength that no cunning or force can undermine it.*

Bauer went into more detail as he read addressed particular points that would be used to ensure success of the plan:

8. *Alcoholic liquors, drugs, moral corruption and vice will be used to corrupt the youth of all nations.*

9. After gaining sufficient power, we have the right to seize property by any means without hesitation.

10. Our slogan, issued to the masses, will be "Liberty, Equality, and Fraternity. [These words became the battle cry of the French Revolution a few years later].

11. *Wars will be directed so that the nations engaged on both sides will be further in debt to our enterprise.*

12. Candidates for public office will be servile and obedient to our commands, so that they might readily be used.

13. *The combined wealth of the organization will control all outlets of public information.*

14. *Contrived and controlled panics and financial depressions will ultimately result in World Government—a new order of one-world government.*

At the end of the meeting the pact was finalized and the plan put into motion.[103]

Mayer Amschel Bauer, adopting the red shield of the coat of arms of Frankfort as his new symbol, changed his family name accordingly to *Rothschild* (Red Shield).

For the next 150 years, the Rothschilds gained wealth, power and influence in every country in Europe. After proper training and guidance, Mayer's five sons established banks in Vienna, Naples, London, Paris, and Frankfort. Each bank, following the original plan formulated in 1773, made its money by loaning operating capital—mostly during times of war and national emergency—to the governments of the respective countries. It was in this fashion that the Rothschilds, who eventually bought out their former partners, gained control over the crowned heads of Europe. By following Mayer's plan, wars were financed on both sides by Rothschild banks, and it made little difference to the bankers who won or lost. Both sides would still owe a collectible debt, in both cash and favors, to the Rothschilds.

One example of playing both sides against the middle came during the Napoleonic War. The Rothschilds had created a system of couriers that could deliver important information between their banks—and subsequently between the heads of state—throughout Europe. Because of the importance of their messages, the couriers, identified by a distinctive red pouch they carried, were granted free passage across borders without fear of being stopped or questioned. Even during fierce battles, when the Rothschild couriers approached, the fighting stopped long enough to let them pass unmolested. For each side knew that the couriers not only carried Rothschild bank documents, but messages between their governments that might influence the war. The Rothschild messengers became the first diplomatic couriers.

During the battle of Waterloo, when Napoleon and his *Grande Armee* faced the Duke of Wellington, Nathan Rothschild sat in the London bond market and watched the trading fluctuate as rumors flew regarding what was happening across the Channel. The English bond speculators realized that if Napoleon won the battle, there would be nothing to keep him from controlling all of Europe—possibly even England. Should that come to pass, the government bonds they possessed would become worthless.

Realizing that the only up-to-date news from the front would arrive with the Rothschild couriers, each investor carefully monitored the reactions of Nathan Rothschild as his messengers arrived with their red pouches and whispered news into his ear. Each time this happened, Rothschild shook his head, looked down and appeared almost to weep. Even between the arrivals of the messengers he looked glum. This could only mean one thing, reasoned the bond-holders: Wellington was losing the battle.

The price of bonds fell drastically by the hour. Large quantities of bonds were dumped on the market, and as it so happens, the value continued to plummet. The more the prices fell, the more gloomy Nathan looked.

Unknown to the English bond holders, Rothschild had agents on the floor buying the English bonds as fast as they were offered. By the time an official English army courier arrived with the news that Wellington had won the Battle of Waterloo, Nathan Rothschild—and the House of Rothschild—owned the British government.[104]

Many books have been written about the Rothschilds rise to power, the international banking cabal, and the secret societies and organizations used by the power brokers to gain and retain control of governments. For the purposes of this work, we will confine ourselves to what has transpired in the two centuries following the American Revolution.

For the student of history and economics, it should be noted that Washington's army was "financed" by banks who created paper money that was not backed by gold or silver. The "Continental Dollar," as the currency was dubbed, was issued only on good faith (much like today's Federal Reserve Notes), and since it was not borrowed from any reputable banking establishment, it contained no provision for the paying of interest to those who created it out of nothing. By the end of 1776, the Continental Dollar commanded only forty cents on the dollar when exchanged for silver coin. Still, the presses cranked the notes out and by 1777 over $240 million worthless Continentals were in circulation. By this time they brought no more than 2.5 cents on the dollar. Two years later they had fallen in value to less than half-a-cent per dollar. By the end of the war it took five hundred paper Continentals to buy one silver dollar.

The situation was so grim that several politicians began to extol the virtues of opening a new "central bank." Such a bank, according to such men as Alexander Hamilton—who felt that average people could not handle their own money and should leave that up to the wealthy who were more fiscally responsible—would be able to control inflation by establishing and maintaining the prime interest rate, the amount of money in circulation, and also be able to loan money to the government. Hamilton proposed that a Bank of the United States, similar in make-up to the Bank of England (the Rothschild bank located in London), would be a profit-making institution that was privately owned, but would have access to public funds. It would have the power to create money out of nothing, and loan it, with interest, to the Federal government.

165

Thomas Jefferson disagreed. "If the American people ever allow private banks to control the issue of currency, first by inflation, then by deflation, the banks and corporations that will grow up around them will deprive the people of their property until their children will wake up homeless on the continent their fathers conquered."[105]

Hamilton, on the other hand, argued that: "No society could succeed which did not unite the interest and credit of rich individuals with those of the state. All communities divide themselves into the few and the many. The first are rich and well-born, the other the mass of people. The people are turbulent and changing; they seldom judge or determine right."[106]

Jefferson responded that the banking establishment, if given the power, would inflate and deflate the quantity of money at will, which in turn creates a "series of oppressions of the people." He wrote that: "single acts of tyranny may be ascribed to the accidental opinion of a day; but a series of oppressions, begun at a distinguished period, and pursued unalterably through every change of ministry, too plainly prove a deliberate systematical plan of reducing us to slavery."

How perceptive.

Unfortunately, George Washington, in 1788, appointed Alexander Hamilton as his Secretary of the Treasury. Three years later the government of the United States granted a twenty year charter to its first civilian-controlled national bank, the First Bank of the United States. Jefferson argued valiantly against the move by Washington and Hamilton, quoting Article I, Section 8, of the Constitution regarding the fact that "The Congress shall have the power to coin money, regulate the value thereof..." and no reference is made to private bankers receiving this privilege. He went on to state that Congress did not have the right or authority to pass this power to any other agency—especially a privately owned entity that could print money that was not backed, then loan it, with interest, to the government.

Jefferson's words fell on deaf ears. But in 1811, when the Bank's first charter lapsed, President James Monroe refused to renew it.

This act on the part of the president was followed just a few months later by yet another war, the War of 1812. Again, the government found that the tax base could not support the conflict at hand and money would have to be borrowed. This would require, according to

Henry Clay and John C. Calhoun, another national bank, "The Second Bank of the United States." Again the banking cartel, ironically "financed" by the Rothschild-controlled Bank of England (who generously loaned money to both sides), won out. This action, within two years, raised the $45 million public debt left over from the Revolution to $127 million.[107]

In 1816, the Second Bank of the United States was re-chartered for twenty years. During this time the bank "loaned" the government a further $60 million, created out of paper bonds that were little more than fancy ink on paper. The interest paid back, however, was in the hard specie of gold and silver. That same year Jefferson again tried to warn the American people—at least those who were literate and capable of influencing politicians—that the entire affair was not only crooked, it was dangerous to the fledgling country. "I believe," he wrote, "that the banking institutions are more dangerous to our liberties than standing armies. Already they have raised up a money aristocracy that has set the Government at defiance. The issuing power should be taken from the banks and restored to the Government, to whom it properly belongs."

This did not happen, and it took until 1834 to pay off the debt incurred during the War of 1812. But by that time the government found itself again in need of further funding due to westward expansion, which required a military force to escort settlers, fight Indians, and take and hold more land. This early "Third World" type of action was followed in 1846 by the Mexican war, and more expansion to the west.

Then came the Civil War.

The Civil War actually started in 1837, the year after the charter of the Second Bank of the United States had expired. It was then that the Rothschilds sent a representative, one August Belmont, to America. After a brief period of buying government bonds and attracting the attention of the White House, Belmont was offered the job of "financial advisor to the President of the United States." The Rothschilds had managed to put a man at the ear of the American president.

For the next ten years the European bankers plotted America's next major emergency—the Civil War. With no chance of the United States being induced into going to war abroad, the only alternative for creating a major requirement for funding by the government which would require government borrowing from the conspirators, would be for the country to go to war against itself. The only problem was how to force this event to occur.

The answer was found in the emotional and volatile issue of slavery.

The critical task to be performed would be to organize a well-financed group to incite the sentiments of the population and force the Union to divide. This was accomplished by forming "The Knights of the Golden Circle"—a overtly racist pro-slavery group organized along the lines of the Ku Klux Klan. This organization, by holding rallies and publishing hate literature and propaganda, began making headway in its crusade in the South as early as 1857, and by 1860 had succeeded in its goal. The southern states, who formed a Confederacy—a group of sovereign countries, each responsible for its own government, army *and* debt—withdrew from the Union in 1860. The rest is history.

What is not history—at least schoolroom history as taught to our children—is the fact that the Rothschilds attempted to finance both sides of the war. But Abraham Lincoln, who could see exactly what was happening, refused to borrow money from the international bankers. Instead, he found a friend and supporter in the one country in Europe not controlled by the Rothschilds: Russia. The Czar, by way of his minister in Washington, pledged support against the British and French who, he assured Lincoln, were the driving forces behind the secession of the South and her subsequent financing. The Russians intervened by providing naval forces for the Union blockade of the South in European waters, and by letting both countries know that if they attempted to join the Confederacy with military forces, they would also have to go to war with Russia. This was a prospect neither country wanted.

Lincoln still needed to finance the Union cause. But instead of borrowing from the international investment bankers by way of a privately owned national central bank, he instead created "Greenbacks," which were printed by the U.S. Treasury—as specified in the original articles of the Constitution.

In retaliation, England sent 8,000 troops to Canada as a show of force for the South, and France dispatched troops to Mexico to bolster emperor Maximillian (who was French). Both efforts were designed in concert to show Lincoln that he was outflanked by the European money powers.

But the show of force, thanks to the Russian threat, failed to sway Lincoln in his handling of financial matters. He still refused to borrow money from the bankers, who he knew would pass the note on to the European banks of the Rothschilds. The Rothschilds, having failed to influence the Federal government with the show of military force, sent a letter to the New York bankers in July, 1862 that addressed the threat of Lincoln's greenbacks to their master plan and mentioned the use of self-generated bonds to secure a federal debt to the bankers:

> "The great debt that capitalists will see to it is made out of the war must be used to control the volume of money. To accomplish this the bonds must be used as a banking basis.
>
> "We are not waiting for the Secretary of the Treasury [Salmon P. Chase] to make this recommendation to Congress.
>
> "It will not do to allow the greenback, as it is called, to circulate as money any length of time, for we cannot control them. But we can control the bonds and through them the bank issues."

The following February the Rothschilds did succeed. By way of their agent, Treasury Secretary Salmon P. Chase, the bankers managed to force a bill through Congress creating a central bank.[108] This act, called the National Banking Act, created a federally chartered bank that had the power to issue U.S. Bank Notes. The notes, designated legal tender by the act, were not backed by gold but by debt, and were loaned to the government at interest.

Lincoln again warned the American people: "The money power preys upon the nation in times of peace and conspires against it in times of adversity. It is more despotic than monarchy, more insolent than autocracy, more selfish than bureaucracy. I see in the near future a crisis approaching that unnerves me, and causes me to tremble for the safety of my country. Corporations have been enthroned, an era of corruption will follow, and the money power of the country will endeavor to prolong its reign by working upon the prejudices of the people, until the wealth is aggregated in a few hands, and the republic is destroyed."[109]

Meanwhile, the Rothschild bank in England sent a letter to its New York representatives that explained: "The few who understand the system will either be so interested in its profits, or so dependent on its favors that there will be no opposition from that class, while on the other hand, the great body of people, mentally incapable of comprehending the tremendous advantages that capital derives from the system, will bear its burdens without complaint, and perhaps without even suspecting the system is inimical to their interests."[110]

Lincoln continued to fight against the central bank, and by 1865 was beginning to make inroads to its demise. It is now believed that his anticipated success in influencing Congress to limit the life of the Bank of the United States to just the war years was the motivating factor behind his assassination. Modern researchers have uncovered evidence of a massive conspiracy that links Lincoln's Secretary of War, Edwin Stanton, to John Wilkes Booth, his eight co-conspirators, and over seventy government officials and businessmen involved in the conspiracy to the Bank of Rothschild. When Booth's diary was recovered by Stanton's troops, it was delivered to Stanton. When it was later produced during the investigation, eighteen pages had been ripped out. These pages, containing the aforesaid names, were later found in the attic of one of Stanton's descendants.

From Booth's trunk, a coded message was found that linked him directly to Judah P. Benjamin, the Civil War campaign manager in the South for the House of Rothschild. When the war ended, the key to the code was found in Benjamin's possession.

The evidence suggests that Lincoln, who posed a roadblock to the master plan of world domination first developed by Amschel Rothschild and being carried out by his sons, was removed from office by a pistol shot. The assassin, portrayed as a crazed lone gunman with a few radical friends, escaped by way of the single bridge in Washington not guarded by Stanton's troops. He was later tracked down, located hiding in a barn, and immediately murdered by troops under Stanton's control—and Stanton certified that the murdered man was Booth.[111] It is now believed that a dupe was used and that the real John Wilkes Booth escaped with Stanton's assistance. It should be noted that Mary Todd Lincoln, upon hearing of her husband's death, began screaming "Oh, that dreadful house!" Earlier historians felt that this spontaneous utterance concerned Lincoln's occupancy of the White House. This author believes the reference was to Thomas W. House, a gun runner, financier, and agent of the Rothschilds during the Civil War who was linked to the anti-Lincoln, pro-banker interests. Thomas W. House was the father of "Colonel" Edward Mandell House, who later became the key player in the election of Woodrow Wilson and the passage of the Federal Reserve Act.

The final act of the Civil War occurred not at Appomattox Court House with the surrender of Lee, but much later, in 1875, when Congress passed the Specie Redemption Act which declared the policy of the government would be to redeem Lincoln's greenbacks for gold. And by this time, over the vociferous objections of the bankers, the central bank had been declared no longer needed. The European money powers had failed once again to establish a grip on the finances of America.

That would change when the next major national emergency occurred: World War I.

Chapter 20

Following the Money

By 1907, the American people—and government—had suffered economic crises caused by the Revolution, the Mexican War, the Civil War, the bank-stimulated panics of 1873 and 1893, the Spanish American War, and finally the Panic of 1907. By this point they were finally conditioned to the point of accepting the solution offered by the money powers: a central banking authority.

In early 1907, Jacob Schiff, the head of the New York investment firm of Kuhn, Loeb & Co.,[112] warned the New York Chamber of Commerce that if a central bank were not instituted, financial chaos would ensue. That same year, a financier named Paul Warburg, sent to the United States by the House of Warburg in Germany—an allied bank of the German branch of the Rothschild Banks—joined Schiff's investment firm. It should be noted that Warburg's brother, Max, ran the family bank in Frankfurt, and would serve as the head of the Kaiser's secret police during World War I.

It is more than coincidental that just after Warburg arrived a major financial panic erupted across the country. It was at this time that New York banker J.P. Morgan—whose father was a gun runner for both sides in the Civil War, and a Rothschild agent for the South—began spreading rumors of insolvencies of competitors banks.[113] This resulted in a bank run by depositors that closed down many of the nations privately-owned banks. Because banks are in the business of loaning money, there are never sufficient funds on hand to cover the balances of all depositors should the majority wish to withdraw funds or close accounts on any given day. The big bankers knew this and planned accordingly.

The 1907 panic caused Congress to establish a National Monetary Commission, a body charged with making "a thorough study of financial practices before formulating banking and currency reform legislation." The Commission, interestingly, was headed by Senator Nelson Aldrich, whose daughter married John D. Rockefeller, Jr., and whose grandson, Nelson Aldrich Rockefeller, became Gerald Ford's vice president in 1974.

Not surprisingly, for their study the Commission went to Europe. For the next two years they toured the banking houses of England, France and Germany—the central banks controlled by the Rothschilds—and returned with a plan.

In November, 1910, Aldrich boarded a private train in Hoboken, New Jersey. His destination was Jekyll Island, Georgia, and a private hunting club owned by J.P. Morgan. Aboard the train were six other men: Benjamin Strong, President of Morgan's Banker's Trust Company; Charles Norton, President of Morgan's First National Bank of New York; Henry Davidson, senior partner of J.P. Morgan; Frank Vanderlip, President of Kuhn-Loeb's National City Bank of New York; A. Piatt Andrew, Assistant Secretary of the Treasury; and of course, Paul Warburg.

Vanderlip later wrote of his role in the coming conspiracy in the *Saturday Evening Post*:

> "I do not feel it is any exaggeration to speak of our secret expedition to Jekyll Island as the occasion of the actual conception of what eventually became the Federal Reserve System.

"We were told to leave our last names behind us. We were told further that we should avoid dining together on the night of our departure. We were instructed to come one at a time and as unobtrusively as possible to the terminal of the New Jersey littoral of the Hudson, where Senator Aldrich's private car would be in readiness, attached to the rear end of the train for the South.

"Once aboard the private car, we began to observe the taboo that had been fixed on last names.

"Discovery, we knew, simply must not happen, or else all our time and effort would be wasted."[114]

The purpose of the meeting was to spend a weekend formulating a plan and writing legislation that would establish a central bank—while avoiding the terminology of "central bank." The legislation, which would be taken to Congress after the conspirators agreed on its content and language, would be written not by legislators, but by a group of bankers that represented J.P. Morgan and the Rothschilds.

The end result was a document in the form of a bill that would eventually establish the Federal Reserve System. It would be operated by private individuals who would draw profit from ownership of shares and who would control the nation's issue of money. Further, the Federal Reserve Board, comprised of twelve districts and one director (the Federal Reserve Chairman), would have the power to control the nation's entire financial resources by setting the interest rate, and would be able to mortgage the government by borrowing money for the United States when the country was forced to participate in major foreign wars.

What the Jekyll Island conspirators had accomplished, at least in design, was a central bank that would be owned by the New York City bankers—who were controlled by the Rothschilds.

But the conspirators had a problem. Their legislation, which would be introduced by Aldrich, would have to pass muster with the President. If the President, William Howard Taft, vetoed the bill, they would have to wait until a new president could be elected that they could control,

174

or at least influence. Taft had already made his sentiments known regarding a central bank, and true to his word, made it clear once the bill was introduced that he would veto it.

The conspirators had to make sure that Taft would not win reelection. But the only way to ensure that would be to run someone against him that could draw enough votes to win against the popular Republican. At first, they supported ex-President Teddy Roosevelt in the Republican primaries. But Roosevelt failed to get the nomination and the race entered the bi-partisan phase. The support of the bankers then fell behind the Democratic contender, Woodrow Wilson. But the polls indicated that Wilson would only draw about 45% of the votes. What the bankers needed was someone that could pull votes away from Taft, someone who could command a sufficient number of Republican votes without harming the Democratic candidate, who by then had promised to sign their bill into law in exchange for their support in the upcoming election.

For this they again turned to Teddy Roosevelt. Roosevelt, a fellow Republican, would run against both men by representing a newly invented third party—his "Bull Moose" party.

The plan worked. Roosevelt succeeded in stealing enough Republican votes from Taft to put Wilson, who had previously agreed to sign the Federal Reserve Bill, in the White House. (The tactic of dividing the votes of the apparent winner so that the minority candidate could be elected was later used in the elections of 1972, 1980 and 1992).

Wilson was inaugurated in January, 1913. He signed the Federal Reserve Bill in December, after it passed the House and Senate.[115] What must be pointed out is that the Bill was held until December 23rd—just two days before Christmas—before it was presented to the House and Senate. Only those senators and congressmen that had not gone home for the holidays—those who owed favors to, or were on the payroll of the bankers—were present to sign the legislation.

Later, Congressman Charles Lindbergh, father of "Lucky Lindy" of the *Spirit of St. Louis* transatlantic flight, stated that the act not only established a huge monopoly, but legalized a powerful invisible government. He, like others before him, attempted to warn the

American people of what had transpired when he wrote that the Federal Reserve Act"...established the most gigantic trust on earth...the invisible government by the money power will be legitimized. The new law will create inflation whenever the trusts want inflation. From now on, depressions will be scientifically created."[116]

Lindbergh hit the nail on the head. The Federal Reserve System was created to foster economic emergencies. For it was only during times of national crises—war or depression—that the government is forced to turn to outside sources for additional funding.

Even Woodrow Wilson, who was forced to borrow money through the Federal Reserve System to finance America's entrance in World War I, felt that he had made a terrible mistake in signing the bill. In his book, *The New Freedom*, he wrote: "Some of the biggest men in the United States, in the field of commerce and manufacture, are afraid of something. They know that there is a power somewhere so organized, so subtle, so watchful, so interlocked, so complete, so pervasive, that they had better not speak above their breath when they speak in condemnation of it."

Besides World War I, the Federal Reserve, using credit provided by the major New York City banks (much of which was Rothschild money), financed every U.S. government emergency to occur in the following years. By the time the country had gone through the Depression, World War II, the Korean conflict, Vietnam, and the Cold War, the U.S. government was in debt to the bankers to the tune of almost $4 trillion dollars!

The privately-owned Federal Reserve is now the nation's largest creditor. In 1989, the interest payments alone on the "National Debt" exceeded $240 Billion—more than half of what the American people pay in federal income taxes! And what is even more frightening, is the fact that the money loaned to the government is no longer backed by gold or silver. For after succeeding in taking the country off of the Gold Standard, the Silver and Gold Certificates issued by the government were replaced by Federal Reserve Notes. And like the Continental Dollar of Washington's era, these notes do not promise redemption in specie. Instead, they simply state that they are "Legal

Tender For All Debts, Public And Private. " In other words, the notes are merely "good faith" bills, created without backing, and loaned to the government at interest. There is no way the international banking cartel could lose with a deal like this.

Lindbergh was not the only legislator to warn of the power transfer created by the Federal Reserve System. Congressmen and Senators, not to mention other members of government, have come forward through the years to expose the ongoing conspiracy behind the nation's economy. Congressman Wright Patman, the Chairman of the House Banking and Currency Committee, said that "In the United States today, we have in effect two governments. We have the duly constituted government, then we have an independent, uncontrolled and un-coordinated government in the Federal Reserve System, operating the money powers which are reserved to Congress by the Constitution."

But these stalwart individuals were few, and far too weak to mount a crusade against the monster that had been created. For every honest politician who saw through the Rothschild plan, a score of others surrendered to the bankers. For in 1980, Congress passed the Monetary Control Act which gave the Federal Reserve System control of *all* depository institutions, whether or not the banks were members of the system.

In only 207 years, Mayer Amschel Rothschild's plan for world domination and "a new order of one world government" was finally succeeding. It is no wonder why the seal on the back side of the one dollar bill which depicts the pyramid, which was built one stone at a time, and the all-seeing eye, bears the inscription "Novus Ordo Seclorum."

New World Order.[2]

---

[2] Literal translation: New Secular (non-religious) Order.

Chapter 21

The Council

On March 26, 1922, John F. Hylan, Mayor of New York City, announced in a speech: "The real menace of our republic is the invisible government which, like a giant octopus, sprawls its slimy length over our city, state and nation. At the head is a small group of banking houses generally referred to as 'international bankers.' This little coterie of powerful international bankers virtually run our government for their own selfish ends."[117]

Then on February 23, 1954, Senator William Jenner warned that "Outwardly we have a Constitutional government. We have operating *within* our government and political system, *another* body representing another form of government, a bureaucratic elite which believes our Constitution is outmoded and is sure that it is the winning side...All the strange developments in foreign policy agreements may be traced to this group who are going to make us over to suit their pleasure."[118]

In modern terminology, this inner circle of power is known as "The Establishment." According to Edith Kermit Roosevelt, granddaughter of President Theodore Roosevelt, "The word 'Establishment' is a general term for the power elite in international finance, business, the professions and government, largely from the northeast, who wield most of the power regardless of who is in the White House. Most people are unaware of the existence of this 'legitimate Mafia.' Yet the power of the Establishment makes itself felt from the professor who seeks a foundation grant, to the candidate for a cabinet post or State Department job. It affects the nation's policies in almost every area."[119]

The "Establishment" referred to by Roosevelt is not confined to the international banking community. Instead, by process of evolution, it incorporates those in big business, investments and the professions. It is mainly made up of old line New England families who have followed traditional career paths that ultimately led to high positions within the government. They attended such schools as Princeton, Harvard, Yale, and Columbia. Many received scholarships abroad—the most influential being the one-world-government oriented Rhodes Scholarship.[120]

The normal progression after attending university is Wall Street. Here, the young elitist either goes into law, as did John J. McCloy, Allen Dulles, John Foster Dulles, and John Mitchell, or into an international investment bank such as Chase Manhattan. Ultimately, he or she may work in both institutions. In any case, those that follow the family ties normally serve a stint in government, typically as a cabinet member, Senator, or administration head. Others may end up in "think tanks" like the Rand Corporation or the Brookings Institute. Many will eventually serve on the boards of such institutions as the Ford, Carnegie or Rockefeller foundations. And a privileged few will enter the Oval Office as President of the United States.

But no matter what career path they follow, no matter who they are or what family they come from, there is a prerequisite for success: membership in the Council on Foreign Relations.

Since its founding in 1921, the Council on Foreign Relations, or CFR, has been the chief link between the eastern money powers and the federal government. Virtually every president was surrounded by members of the CFR, and almost every president since that year has been a member.

The Council, which serves efficiently as a front organization for the Establishment and a clandestine contact point between U.S. government officials and foreign powers, has been called "The heart of the

American Establishment." Within its membership rolls are such names as Rockefeller, Morgan, Peabody, Stimson, McCloy, Dulles, Harriman, Vanderbilt, Nixon, Kissinger, Carter, Oppenheimer, Westmoreland, McNamara, Bush and Clinton.

The *Christian Science Monitor* observed in September, 1961, that "there is a constant flow of its members from private life to public service. Almost half of the council members have been invited to assume official government positions or to act as consultants at one time or another."

According to Pat Robertson in his book, *The New World Order*, "The power of the Establishment is beyond question. Since 1940 every United States secretary of state except one (former Governor James Byrnes of South Carolina) has been a CFR member. And since 1940, all secretaries of war/defense, from Henry L. Stimson through Richard Cheney, have been CFR members."

The success of the Council in infiltrating the highest circles of government is not a phenomenon. It was planned that way from its earliest of days. In a *New York Times* article written by Anthony Lukas in 1971, the fraternity syndrome of the CFR was exhibited:

> Everyone knows how fraternity brothers can help other brothers climb the ladder of life. If you want to make foreign policy, there's no better fraternity to belong to than the Council.
>
> When Henry Stimson—the group's quintessential member—went to Washington in 1940 as Secretary of War, he took with him John McCloy, who was to become Assistant Secretary in charge of personnel. McCloy has recalled: "Whenever we needed a man we thumbed through the roll of Council members and put though a call to New York."

And over the years, the men McCloy called in turn called other Council members.

The Council's origins can be traced back much farther than its published beginnings. In fact it can be traced back to the original Round Table Group of elitists founded by Cecil Rhodes. On February 5, 1891, the Round Table Group, known to those chosen for membership as "the Inner Circle," was formed in London by Rhodes, Lord Curzon, Lord Rothschild, and Lord Rosebery (Rothschild's son-in-law). By 1899, the Round Table Group had members across the Atlantic and became known as "The British-American Secret Society." According to Dr. Carrol Quigley in his book, *Tragedy and Hope*, "The chief backbone of this organization grew up along the already existing financial cooperation running from the Morgan Bank in New York to a group of international financiers in London led by the Lazar Brothers [and the Rothschilds]."

In 1899, J.P. Morgan went to England to attend the International Bankers Convention. By the time he returned, he had been appointed head representative of the Rothschild interests in the United States. In *Pawns In The Game*, William Guy Carr points out that "As a result of the London Conference, J.P. Morgan and Company of New York, Drexel and Company of Philadelphia, Grenfell and Company of London, and Morgan Harges Cie of Paris, M.M. Warburg Company of Germany and America, and the House of Rothschild were all affiliated."

After World War I, the Round Table Group was renamed. In London, it became the Royal Institute of International Affairs. In the U.S., it became the Council on Foreign Relations.

And both were controlled by the London branch of the House of Rothschild.

What exactly is the goal of the CFR? By controlling the banks and the Federal Reserve, the members of the CFR have secured the true power above even that of the U.S. government, and by doing so have managed to reap the fortunes such power would bring. They have also been the driving factor behind the formation of the United Nations, an international police force, and a one-world economy interdependent on each nation's monetary stability. And they have managed to direct

181

foreign policy for not only the United States, but every super power in the world including Russia.

But those are only partial goals. The actual objective of the Council on Foreign Relations is the creation of a one-world government, backed by a one-world monetary unit. This would require reducing national governments to a level of servitude below, for lack of a better term, "The World Council." The new global authority could then become the centralized government and single power over all the world's formerly independent nations. This is exactly the goal Mayer Amschel Rothschild had in mind when he formed his secret pact with his twelve disciples in Frankfort in 1773.

The CFR itself has given its hand away on several occasions in articles printed in its journal *Foreign Affairs*. In the December, 1922 issue, the magazine declared:

> "Obviously there is going to be no peace or prosperity for mankind so long as it remains divided into fifty or sixty independent states...Equally obviously there is going to be no steady progress in civilization or self-government among the more backward peoples until some kind of international system is created which will put an end to the diplomatic struggles incident to the attempt of every nation to make itself secure...The real problem today is that of world government."

Then in 1944, the Council published a paper titled "American Public Opinion and Post-war Security Commitments" that reported to its members that: "The sovereignty fetish is still so strong in the public mind, that there would appear to be little chance of winning popular assent to American membership in anything approaching a super-state organization. Much will depend on the kind of approach which is used in further popular education."

The Council, by this time, realized that to reach a goal of one-world government, they would have to become involved in education of the young. For as Hitler stated in 1939, "When an opponent declares: 'I will not come over to your side,' I calmly say, 'your child belongs to us already. What are you? You will pass on. Your descendants, however, now stand in the new camp. In a short time they will know nothing else but this new community."

Education of the young was, and remains, the key to influencing future generations into accepting world government. Only by removing current nationalistic—and family—values can the plan for world domination succeed.

America was founded on Christian principles of a society that centered around the family. But over the years, these values have eroded. In great part, the process of erosion was facilitated by court rulings that favored minority lawsuits. The 1963 ruling removing prayer from the classroom, upheld by the Earl Warren Supreme Court concerning the lawsuit filed by atheist leader Madalyn Murray O'Hair, serves as one example of a systematic loss of individual freedoms.

After decades of such actions, the basis of public education has changed drastically. Critics say that "The aim of education is no longer to impart facts and knowledge...The aim is to change the social values of the child away from values that have traditionally been considered fixed, permanent and absolute."[121] This falls in line with ideology presented by "educator" John Dewey when he stated that the schools should: "Take an active part in determining the social order of the future as the teachers align themselves with the forces making for social control of economic forces."[122] Dewey, who never taught young students himself, but instead concentrated on teaching teachers, began teaching in the educational disciplines at Columbia University in 1904. Today, twenty percent of all American school superintendents and forty percent of all teacher college heads have advanced degrees from Columbia.[123]

Dewey also taught four of the five Rockefeller brothers, including David and Nelson.[124]

John D. Rockefeller, grand patriarch of the Rockefeller clan, founded the General Education Board, forerunner of today's Rockefeller Foundation. Its purpose was to gain control of, and eventually change, the American educational system to meet the requirements of the power elite. This would be accomplished by means of controllable grants and specialized training for educators, who would then spread the new ideologies of liberalism and globalism throughout the rest of the country's educational systems. The first manifestation of this effort concentrated in the eastern Ivy League universities, then after gaining a solid foundation, infiltrated other major school systems across the country.

The plan's success was phenomenal. Frederick T. Gates, chairman of Rockefeller's original GEB, wrote: "...we have limitless resources and the people yield themselves with perfect docility to our molding hands. The present educational conventions fade from our minds and, unhampered by tradition, we work our will upon a grateful and responsive rural folk."[125]

Whether or not the "rural folk" were grateful or responsive is yet to be seen. What is known, however, is that since the GEB's incursion into the American educational system, the choices of schools and curriculum for children by their parents have decreased. The government educational bureaucracies, following the guidance of the Rockefeller Foundation, have strived to eliminate the only remaining alternative to public education: private schools. As an example, on May 20, 1979, the Supreme Court ruled against legislation that gave parents a tax break should they decide to enroll their children in a private school. They would be forced to pay for two educations, both public and private, even though they opted to use only the later.

According to author A. Ralph Epperson, the objectives of the decades-old educational master plan are being carried out by the Rockefeller Foundation-supported National Education Association (NEA) and are exhibited in the strong positions the NEA have taken:

1. Educate the youth for a global community.
2. Promote a stronger United Nations.
3. Promote the Declaration of *Interdependence* (where nations are totally dependant on each other).
4. Oppose tuition tax credits.
5. Support a National Health Plan (socialized medicine).
6. Oppose any legislation to benefit private schools.

7. The basics (reading, writing, mathematics, history, civics and geography) should not occupy more than one quarter of the student's time.
8. Support population control (abortion).
9. Promote and teach Secular Humanism (Non-singular God religion where the "enlightenend Man" is actually godlike).
10. Promote and support federal day-care centers.
11. Support increased federal aid and control of education.
12. Oppose local control of public schools.
13. Oppose local financing of public schools.
14. Oppose parental supervision of textbooks.
15. Oppose taxation programs that remove the obligation for payment of taxes from homeowners who send their children to private schools.
16. Oppose tuition tax credits for parents who pay for both a public and private education.[126]

It is in these tenets that the youth of America are being programmed for their part in the globalist society envisioned by Mayer Amschel Rothschild in 1773, the international government referred to today as the New World Order.

Chapter 22

The Power

A very successful preacher once said that to properly tell a story, one must: "Tell em' what you're gonna say, then say it, then tell 'em what you just said." These are astute words indeed, for they exhibit what every successful writer knows. A story must have a beginning, a middle, and an end—and when possible, the end should form a complete circle in which it reflects the beginning. If there was a question asked in the beginning, it should be answered in the end.

In this closing chapter the assassination of John F. Kennedy, which began this book, must be revisited. For it was in the introduction that the questions were asked concerning who could have ordered his death, who would have benefitted, and who had the power to cover the conspiracy up for over four decades. Questions were also asked concerning the existence of some unseen power behind—or above—the national government. By exposing the diabolical behind-the-scenes activities and secret histories of many organizations both within, and outside of, the U.S. government, we have seen that murdering one man, regardless of his position, was considered little more than business as usual.

The "Power" alluded to in the introduction has been identified. The secret societies and councils that have emanated from the original Rothschild conspiracy, as shown in the preceding pages, are the powers behind not only the U.S. Government, but every major government in the world today. Their objective, the ultimate end to Rothschild's plan, is a one-world government that has dominion over all nations. Of necessity, this global entity must have a one world monetary system, a global military police force, and a single anti-Christian humanist religion.[127]

The foot soldiers for the globalists, as we have seen, have consistently been the clandestine intelligence services. In modern times, the clandestine services in this country have ranged from General William "Wild Bill" Donovan's Office of Strategic Services (OSS), through Allen Dulles's follow-on Central Intelligence Group (CIG), to the Central Intelligence Agency. Accompanying these organizations, when the scope of a given operation exceeded the assets of the covert community, were elements of small, elite military organizations such as the U.S. Army Special Forces, U.S. Air Force Air Commandos, and U.S. Navy SEALs.

And when "National Security" was considered to be a cover for an operation, no law or morals stood in the way of the mission. From the ruins of of Nazi Germany, where war criminals were spirited away from prosecution by the thousands in such covert operations as Paperclip and Omega and by certain high-ranking individuals within the OSS (each supplied by the CFR), to traitorous handling of the war in Korea through the U.N., to the manipulations and assassinations of the leadership of Third World countries during the Cold War Years, through the financial and political manipulations of the Vietnam War, Watergate, Iran/Contra, Desert Shield/Storm, Somalia, and Bosnia, to today, the moral values of the shadow warriors and the entities that control them have been shown to be non-existent. And in the years following World War II, through the Cold War, the financing of the rebuilding of Germany and Japan, and all of the above stepping stones of history, the same powers and covert organizations have continued to move in one direction: toward more power and influence. It did not matter if crimes had to be perpetrated and covered up, whether the players violated every law and moral code written, whether men supplied by the masses, such as those who fought in the Civil War, World War I, World War II, Korea and Vietnam, had to be sacrified to meet the goals of the secret agenda, as long as the final objective was attained. And herein lies the key that opens the door to the mysteries of the present, for no one can remain a criminal without eventual discovery. And when that discovery occurs, it is like opening Pandora's Box.

Only by linking together the players and the organizations involved in the stories told on these pages can one see the continuity of people and events. Multitudes of men like John J. McCloy, Averill Harriman, and Henry Kissinger, all of whom held more positions of power in their political careers than did virtually any president of the United States, seemed to lurk in the background ever since the Revolution. But few have been previously exposed for what they really were: agents of the Power Elite and pawns in the Rothschild Plan. Even during the administration of John F. Kennedy, who was the only president since 1921 who refused membership in the inner circle when offered, the cabinet was filled with representatives of the conspirators. There is little room for maneuvering when one is surrounded by the enemy.

Many motives have been offered through the years for the death of John F. Kennedy. A few, upon study, are valid up to a point. Of these, there are:

1. The anti-Castro Cubans, who, assisted by former CIA controllers, avenged the Bay of Pigs debacle;

2. The CIA, who if Kennedy was eliminated, would remain intact instead of being "scattered to the winds" as Kennedy threatened;

3. The Mafia, who wished to "get rid of the Kennedy boys" who were causing them so many problems, and finally,

4. The Military/Industrial/Banking complex that stood so much to gain from the escalating war in Vietnam—from which Kennedy had announced the U.S. was withdrawing.

5. Lyndon Johnson and his Texas backers who had so much to gain from the War in Vietnam and the power the presidency brings.

But even though the plot would, to a certain extent, require the cooperation of selected elements of each of these entities, the most important motive is not on this list.

Kennedy's death could not be attributed solely to the Cubans, the CIA, the Mafia, or the M/I/B complex. Instead, the reason behind the decision to eliminate the president was something far more important to the conspirators than revenge or war profits: President John F. Kennedy, like Lincoln before him, was about to interfere with the progress of the master plan. After two hundred years of alternating victories and setbacks for the international banking cabal, and just when they had total power within their grasp by way of controlling the nation's economy, *Kennedy planned to exterminate the Federal Reserve System, then put the country back on the Gold Standard.* In this action he would put the country back on a cash-and-carry basis, get away from deficit spending, and eventually eliminate the national debt—as had Andrew Jackson and Abraham Lincoln before him when they did the same to the two Rothschild-organized central banks!

In 1963, by presidential order of John F. Kennedy (EO 11 and EO 110), the United States Treasury began printing over $4 billion worth of "United States Notes" to replace Federal Reserve Notes. When a sufficient supply of these notes entered circulation, the Federal Reserve Notes—and hence, the Federal Reserve Board—would have been declared obsolete. This done, the notes printed and issued by the Federal Reserve Board would have been removed from circulation as they wore out and would no longer be issued. This, in effect, would end the control of the international investment bankers over the U.S. government—and the American people.

For those in doubt, a few of these bills can still be found. They can be recognized easily by the distinctive *red* seal on the front of the bill in lieu of the green seal of the Federal Reserve Notes. At the top of the bills, above the portrait of the $2 dollar and $5 dollar notes that were printed, are the words "United States Note." No mention is made of the Federal Reserve. The series is 1963 and C. Douglas Dillon's signature appears as Secretary of the Treasury. The reverse of these bills is identical to the Federal Reserve notes.[128]

It can now be seen why Kennedy was murdered. Should his plan have been permitted to succeed, the international banking cabal—and the Rothschild plan—would have been set back indefinitely. This prospect was unacceptable. The only solution would be to remove Kennedy from office immediately—before he could do irreparable damage to everything the generations of globalists had built. It was a matter of survival.

For the shadow organizations who had plotted Lincoln's assassination, the takeover of the nation's money system, the assassination attempts of Fidel Castro by the ZR/RIFLE team, the coups against Allende of Chile, Arbenz of Guatemala, and Mossadegh of Iran, the elimination of over 25,000 Vietnamese during Operation Phoenix, and other hits carried out during the CIA's Executive Action operations, it was "business as usual"

The decision was made, the orders given. The result was an ambush in Dealey Plaza by assassins provided by the same organizations who had served the money powers for decades: selected cells within the clandestine intelligence community. The same people, under the same leadership, that maneuvered around the law to accomplish whatever they were called upon to do by The Power, all under the guise of National Security, were on center stage for another operation to eliminate a threat to their private agenda: John F. Kennedy.

No entity lower than the Rothschild Plan conspirators could have ordered such an operation, planned it, executed it, then managed to cover it up for three decades. Neither the anti-Castro Cuban community, nor the Mafia, the military, or even the industrialists could have manipulated the White House (Lyndon Johnson), the Warren Commission, the CIA, and the FBI in the investigation of the assassination, then continued to ensure an ongoing program to suppress evidence, eliminate witnesses, and hide from the public the original investigative records until the year 2029. No single individual, governmental agency, or administration has that amount of continuous power.

That kind of omnipotence resides solely in The Power Elite.

SINISTER PURPOSE

After decades of deception, it can now be seen that the emperor, no matter how he has attempted to hide the fact, wears no clothes. The crimes committed, the insidious plotting and Machiavellian maneuvering, have resulted in the exposure of the entity that has, for over two centuries, endeavored to maintain invisibility as it stretched its tentacles into every office of power and influence in the world.

In its wake, the serpent of conspiracy has left behind a legacy of lies, theft, bribery, manipulation—and murder. For the people of the world, it has left a legacy of dishonor that made its most graphic public appearance in a kill zone called Dealey Plaza.

And the Serpent lives on...

The man in the street does not notice the devil even when the devil is holding him by the throat.

Johann von Goethe

Go to now, ye rich men, weep and howl for your miseries that shall come upon you. Your riches are corrupted, and your garments are motheaten. Your gold and silver is cankered; and the rust of them shall be a witness against you, and shall eat your flesh as it were fire. Ye have heaped treasure together for the last days.

James 5:1-3

ILLUSTRATIONS

AND

APPENDIX

POINTS OF CROSSFIRE IN THE AMBUSH ZONE

NORTH

TEAM 2

DalTex Bldg

TEAM 3

Dallas County Records Bldg

ELM

Dallas County Court Bldg

MAIN

HOUSTON

TEXAS SCHOOLBOOK DEPOSITORY

Diversionary Team

Back Shot (Sabot)

Cranium Shot

Diversionary Shot

Diversionary Shot Missed

Throat Shot

Head Shot

Missed Shot-Wounds Tague

TEAM 1

Grassy Knoll

"Railroad Man"

193

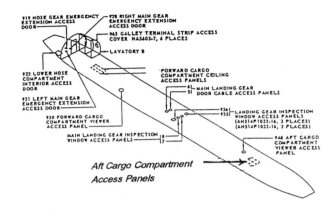

Aft Cargo Compartment
Access Panels

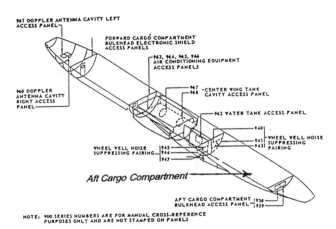

Aft Cargo Compartment

NOTE: 900 SERIES NUMBERS ARE FOR MANUAL CROSS-REFERENCE PURPOSES ONLY AND ARE NOT STAMPED ON PANELS

CUTAWAY VIEWS OF 720 AND 707 SERIES AIRCRAFT SHOWING AVAILABLE ACCESS PANELS AND DOORS

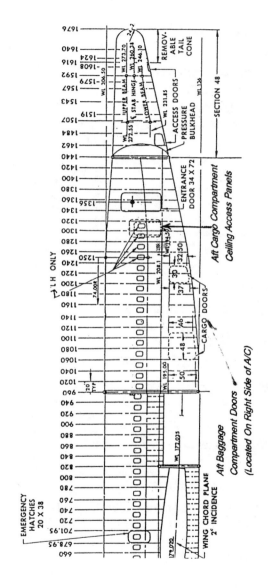

INTERIOR DOORS AND ACCESS PANELS
(720 And 707 Series aircraft)

195

FORMER FIRST FAMILY MEMBERS AWAIT THE REMOVAL OF LBJ'S
CASKET FROM AIR FORCE ONE--TAIL NUMBER 26000--ON 24
JANUARY, 1972. NOTE THE ABSENCE OF THE TAIL "VENTRAL
FIN" BENEATH EMPENAGE SECTION.

DEPARTMENT OF THE AIR FORCE
HEADQUARTERS 89TH AIRLIFT WING (MAC)
ANDREWS AIR FORCE BASE. WASHINGTON. D.C 20331-5000

6 Apr 92

Dear Mr. Roberts,

Thank you for your letter. I hope I can answer your questions. First let me say that I should have told you that I am not extremely happy with the way that book was written. I'm in the process of writing a sequel to that one which will hopefully give a little more in-depth information on the past aircraft of this wing.

Let me start by assuring you that there was only one aircraft with the tail #26000. It was delivered to the 1254th Air Transport Wing on 10 October 1962 as a C-137C. (Boeing 707-320). It was originally built with the ventral fin attached but as part of a modification in 1968, the ventral fin was removed. Other modifications included leading edge flaps, new wing tips, take-off flaps from 17 to 14 degrees, and larger sucker doors. Interior modifications were a result of President Johnson requesting that the State Room be relocated to the front of the aircraft as well as the entry/exit door.

You were correct in stating that the first three C-137s were Boeing 707-120 models. (They were later modified in 1963 to C-137Bs and are still being used in the 89th Airlift Wing, 1st Airlift Squadron). They were originally delivered as follows:

C-137	#58-6970	12 May 59
C-137	#58-6971	30 May 59
C-137	#58-6972	30 Jun 59
C-137C	#62-6000	10 Oct 62
C-137C	#72-7000	23 Dec 72

Aircraft #26000 was the aircraft that transported both President Kennedy and Johnson's body. 6970 did not do this. Although 6970 was used by President Kennedy on several occasions, it was never officially designated as the Presidential Aircraft. By the way, no aircraft is called "Air Force One". This is only a call sign given to whatever aircraft has the president on board at the time, and "Air Force Two" is the call sign when the Vice President is on board. Just one of the many problems with the book I sent you. On Friday, 3 Apr 92, President Bush came out to the base and departed Andrews on a Gulfstream C-20 at which time it was designated "Air Force One." So it is rather difficult to get the idea across that AF-1 is not a plane. Currently, the official presidential aircraft is #28000 with #29000 as its backup, both Boeing 747-200B's with the Air Force designation of VC-25A. PROUD MAC — SUPPORT AMERICA CAN ALWAYS COUNT ON

*REPLY LETTER FROM ANDREWS AFB REGARDING
LINEAGE OF AIR FORCE ONE AND 89TH AW AIRPLANES*

I have listed for you all assigned aircraft to the 89th
Airlift Wing by Tail Number. As you can see, all of the
previously mentioned aircraft are still assigned to the
wing.

AIRCRAFT ASSIGNED TO THE 89TH AIRLIFT WING

TYPE		TAIL #
2	VC-25A	28000 / 29000
4	C-137C	56973 / 56974 / 26000 / 27000
3	C-137B	86970 / 86971 / 86972
2	C-135B	*24126 /*24127
**2	C-135B - Det 1	24130 / 12668
3	C-9C	31681 / 31682 / 31683
7	C-20B	60200 / 60201 / 60202 / 60203 / 60204
		60205 / 60206
3	C-20C	50049 / 50050 / 60403
2	C-12C	31213 / 63239
19	UH-1N Heli's	

---

47 Total

*   AC C-135B #24127 was turned over to SAC on 26 Sep 91
*   AC C-135B #24126 was turned over to USAFE on 1 Oct 91
** Detachment One, Hickam AFB, Hawaii, was reassigned to
    PACAF on 10 March 1992.

   (The present number of aircraft assigned to the 89th is
   now 43).

I hope I have answered some of your questions. If there is
anything I missed or you have other questions, please
contact me anytime. (301) 981-2829

Sincerely,

THOMAS E. PENNINGTON, MSgt, USAF
Historian

WHILE LBJ WAS BEING SWORN IN AS PRESIDENT
ABOARD AIR FORCE ONE (26000), KENNEDY'S
BODY WAS BEING REMOVED FROM CASKET IN AFT
GALLEY AREA AND DROPPED INTO AFT CARGO
COMPARTMENT THROUGH ACCESS PANELS IN FLOOR.
THIS WAS THE ONLY TIME THE CASKET WAS LEFT
UNATTENDED. BY THE TIME AIR FORCE ONE TOOK
OFF FROM DALLAS, THE CASKET WAS EMPTY.

260

AS THE EMPTY CASKET IS BEING REMOVED IN THE LIGHTED
AREA TO THE LEFT OF AIR FORCE ONE, THE BODY IS BEING
REMOVED (PROBABLY INSIDE A BODY BAG OR ALUMINUM
SHIPPING CASKET) FROM THE RIGHT SIDE CARGO COMPARTMENT,
IN THE DARK, TO A WAITING HELICOPTER WHICH IMMEDIATELY
TAKES OFF FOR WALTER REED--WHERE THE BODY WAS MODIFIED
TO ELIMINATE PHYSICAL EVIDENCE OF THE TRAJECTORY OF
THE HEAD SHOT AND THROAT WOUND. (NOTE VENTRAL FIN
TO THE RIGHT OF GANTRY TRUCK, UNDER TAIL SECTION)

. . .At 1100 hours on 21 November, President Kennedy, his wife Jacqueline, personal entourage, and accompanying press media, left Andrews on a non-stop flight to Dallas, Texas, for what was termed by the White House as a "Non-political tour of the southwest." Press media on hand for the departure included the Associated Press, United Press International, NBC-TV, and CBS-TV. . .Following the assassination of the President in the early afternoon of 22 November (Friday), the body of John F. Kennedy arrived at Andrews at 1808 the same evening, accompanied by his widow; newly sworn-in President Lyndon B. Johnson, and his wife ladybird. . .The Air Terminal area was jammed with thousands of people, including the largest gathering of press and TV media ever assembled at anytime before in the history of Andrews Air Force Base.   At plane-side, shortly after the body of the slain President was removed to Walter Reed General Hospital, President Johnson spoke briefly on the great loss of the 35th President of the United States and in closing, said, Part: "I will do my best. That is all I can do." In the following three days, numerous officers and airmen from this Base took part in the various funeral activities held at the White House, Capitol, St. Matthew's Cathedral, and the Arlington National Cemetery where the late President's body was buried; watched by millions of mourners from all walks of life, in person and via life television. . . Thus ended a chapter in the life of a very colorful national figure; always hatless, always smiling; waving on several occasions to persons standing in the roped-off "press" section at plane-side-every time he arrived on base in a Helicopter from the White House - to depart in the VC-137C Presidential aircraft.

PAGE EXCERPT FROM "THE HISTORY OF ANDREWS AIR FORCE BASE" SHOWING ORIGNIAL ENTRY THAT JFK'S BODY WAS REMOVED TO <u>WALTER REED GENERAL HOSPITAL</u>. THIS WAS LATER CHANGED TO REFLECT BETHESDA WHEN HISTORY WAS REWRITTEN TO LEAVE OUT THIS "ERROR."

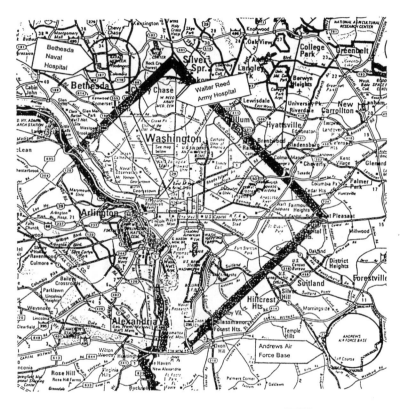

MAP OF WASHINGTON D.C. SHOWING THE RELATIVE DISTANCES
BETWEEN ANDREWS AIR FORCE BASE, WALTER REED ARMY
HOSPITAL, AND BETHESDA NAVAL HOSPITAL.

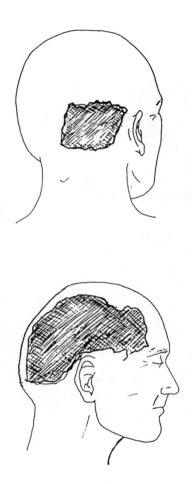

COMPLETELY DIFFERENT DESCRIPTIONS
OF KENNEDY'S HEAD WOUND. PARKLAND
(TOP) AND BETHESDA (BOTTOM).

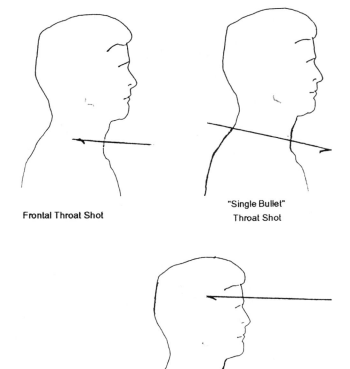

Frontal Throat Shot

"Single Bullet"
Throat Shot

Actual Direction
Of Wounds

DOCTORS AT PARKLAND SAW A FRONTAL ENTRANCE WOUND TO
THROAT. BETHESDA DOCTORS SAW AN ENTRANCE WOUND IN
THE BACK AND A LARGE GASH IN THE THROAT. WARREN
COMMISSION RAISED REAR WOUND TO NECK TO ACCOMADATE
"SINGLE BULLET THEORY."

204

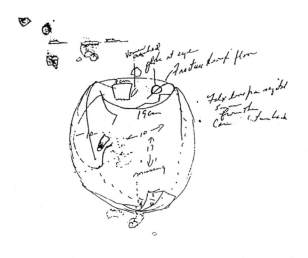

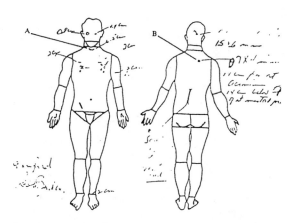

AUTOPSY SKETCHES FROM BETHESDA DOCTORS SHOW
SHALLOW BULLET ENTRANCE WOUND DOWN ON BACK,
TO THE RIGHT OF SPINE.

The Chairman. Of course there are so many Spanish-speaking people down in Texas.

Mr. Rankin. In the area.

The Chairman. That she might have gotten it from someone else.

Mr. Rankin. Then there is a great range of material in regard to the wounds, and the autopsy and this point of exit or entrance of the bullet in the front of the neck, and that all has to be developed much more than we have at the present time.

We have an explanation there in the autopsy that probably a fragment came out the front of the neck, but with the elevation the shot must have come from, and the angle, it seems quite apparent now, since we have the picture of where the bullet entered in the back, that the bullet entered below the shoulder blade to the right of the backbone, which is below the place where the picture shows the bullet came out in the neckband of the shirt in front, and the bullet, according to the autopsy didn't strike any bone at all, that particular bullet, and go through.

So that how it could turn and --

Rep. Boggs. I thought I read that bullet just went in a finger's length.

Mr. Rankin. That is what they first said. They reached in and they could feel where it came, it didn't go any further than that, about part of the finger or something, part of the autopsy, and then they proceeded to reconstruct where they thought

TOP SECRET

EXTRACT OF WARREN COMMISSION TRANSCRIPT DESCRIBING BULLET WOUND TO KENNEDY'S BACK. THIS LETTER ALONE DESTROYS BOTH SPECTER'S AND POSNER'S "MAGIC BULLET" THEORY.

~~TOP SECRET~~ - EYES ONLY   October 11, 1963

NATIONAL SECURITY ACTION MEMORANDUM NO. 263

TO: Secretary of State
           Secretary of Defense
           Chairman of the Joint Chiefs of Staff

SUBJECT: South Vietnam

At a meeting on October 5, 1963, the President considered the
recommendations contained in the report of Secretary McNamara
and General Taylor on their mission to South Vietnam.

The President approved the military recommendations contained
in Section I B (1-3) of the report, but directed that no formal
announcement be made of the implementation of plans to withdraw 1, 000 U.S. miltitary personnel by the end of 1963.

After discussion of the remaining recommendations of the report,
the President approved an instruction to Ambassador Lodge which
is set forth in State Department telegram No. 534 to Saigon.

                                        McGeorge Bundy

Copy furnished:
    Director of Central Intelligence
    Administrator, Agency for International Development

                                   cc:
                                       Mr. Bundy ✓
                                       Mr. Forrestal
                                       Mr. Johnson
                   ~~TOP SECRET - EYES ONLY~~ NSC Files

Committee Print of Pentagon Papers
BY HS2   DATE 7/15/77

**NATIONAL SECURITY MEMORANDUM 263 SIGNED BY
MCGEORGE BUNDY FOR JFK REGARDING VIETNAM PULLOUT**

November 26, 1963

NATIONAL SECURITY ACTION MEMORANDUM NO. 273

TO: The Secretary of State
           The Secretary of Defense
           The Director of Central Intelligence
           The Administrator, AID
           The Director, USIA

The President has reviewed the discussions of South Vietnam which
occurred in Honolulu, and has discussed the matter further with
Ambassador Lodge. He directs that the following guidance be issued
to all concerned:

1. It remains the central object of the United States in South
Vietnam to assist the people and Government of that country to win
their contest against the externally directed and supported Communist
conspiracy. The test of all U. S. decisions and actions in this area
should be the effectiveness of their contribution to this purpose.

2. The objectives of the United States with respect to the withdrawal
of U. S. military personnel remain as stated in the White House statement of October 2, 1963.

3. It is a major interest of the United States Government that the
present provisional government of South Vietnam should be assisted
in consolidating itself and in holding and developing increased public
support. All U. S. officers should conduct themselves with this
objective in view.

4. The President expects that all senior officers of the Government
will move energetically to insure the full unity of support for established
U. S. policy in South Vietnam. Both in Washington and in the field, it
is essential that the Government be unified. It is of particular importance
that express or implied criticism of officers of other branches be
scrupulously avoided in all contacts with the Vietnamese Government
and with the press. More specifically, the President approves the
following lines of action developed in the discussions of the Honolulu
meeting of November 20. The offices of the Government to which
central responsibility is assigned are indicated in each case.

                         TOP SECRET   (page 1 of 3 pages)

JOHNSON'S NSM 273 DATED NOVEMBER 26TH
WRITTEN BY MCGEORGE BUNDY FOR LBJ'S
POLICY TO COMMIT FORCES AND AID TO
SOUTH VIETNAM.

5. We should concentrate our own efforts, and insofar as possible we should persuade the Government of South Vietnam to concentrate its efforts, on the critical situation in the Mekong Delta. This concentration should include not only military but political, economic, social, educational and informational effort. We should seek to turn the tide not only of battle but of belief, and we should seek to increase not only the control of hamlets but the productivity of this area, especially where the proceeds can be held for the advantage of anti-Communist forces.

(Action: The whole country team under the direct supervision of the Ambassador.)

6. Programs of military and economic assistance should be maintained at such levels that their magnitude and effectiveness in the eyes of the Vietnamese Government do not fall below the levels sustained by the United States in the time of the Diem Government. This does not exclude arrangements for economy on the MAP account with respect to accounting for ammunition, or any other readjustments which are possible as between MAP and other U. S. defense resources. Special attention should be given to the expansion of the import, distribution, and effective use of fertilizer for the Delta.

(Action: AID and DOD as appropriate.)

7. Planning should include different levels of possible increased activity, and in each instance there should be estimates of such factors as:

A. Resulting damage to North Vietnam;

B. The plausibility of denial;

C. Possible North Vietnamese retaliation;

D. Other international reaction.

Plans should be submitted promptly for approval by higher authority. (Action: State, DOD, and CIA.)

8. With respect to Laos, a plan should be developed and submitted for approval by higher authority for military operations up to a line up to 50 kilometers inside Laos, together with political plans for minimizing the international hazards of such an enterprise. Since it is agreed that operational responsibility for such undertakings should

TOP SECRET   (page 2 of 3 pages)

pass from CAS to MACV, this plan should include a redefined method of political guidance for such operations, since their timing and character can have an intimate relation to the fluctuating situation in Laos.

(Action: State, DOD, and CIA.)

9. It was agreed in Honolulu that the situation in Cambodia is of the first importance for South Vietnam, and it is therefore urgent that we should lose no opportunity to exercise a favorable influence upon that country. In particular a plan should be developed using all available evidence and methods of persuasion for showing the Cambodians that the recent charges against us are groundless.

(Action: State.)

10. In connection with paragraphs 7 and 8 above, it is desired that we should develop as strong and persuasive a case as possible to demonstrate to the world the degree to which the Viet Cong is controlled, sustained and supplied from Hanoi, through Laos and other channels. In short, we need a more contemporary version of the Jorden Report, as powerful and complete as possible.

(Action: Department of State with other agencies as necessary.)

b !

McGeorge Bundy

~~TOP SECRET~~

NATIONAL SECURITY ACTION MEMORANDUM NO. _____

The President has reviewed the discussions of South Vietnam which occurred in Honolulu, and has discussed the matter further with Ambassador Lodge. He directs that the following guidance be issued to all concerned:

1. It remains the central object of the United States in South Vietnam to assist the people and Government of that country to win their contest against the externally directed and supported Communist conspiracy. The test of all decisions and U. S. actions in this area should be the effectiveness of their contribution to this purpose.

2. The objectives of the United States with respect to the withdrawal of U. S. military personnel remain as stated in the White House statement of October 2, 1963.

3. It is a major interest of the United States Government that the present provisional government of South Vietnam should be assisted in consolidating itself and in holding and developing increased public support. All U. S. officers should conduct themselves with this objective in view.

4. It is of the highest importance that the United States Government avoid either the appearance or the reality of public recrimination from one part of it against another, and the President expects that all senior officers of the Government will take energetic steps to insure that they and their

~~TOP SECRET~~

DRAFT COPY OF NSM 273 WRITTEN BY MCGEORGE BUNDY FOR LBJ ON NOVEMBER 21ST--THE DAY BEFORE KENNEDY WAS ASSASSINATED.

211

Directors, Central Intelligence Agency

Office of Strategic Services (OSS)

1940-45 William J. "Wild Bill" Donovan (CFR: 1931)

Central Intelligence Group (CIG)

1946   Rear Adm Sidney Souers
1946-47 Gen Walter Bedell Smith (CFR: 1949)

Central Intelligence Agency

1947-50 Rear Adm. Roscoe H. Hillenkoetter
1950-53 Gen. Walter Bedell Smith (CFR: 1949)
1953-61 Allen W. Dulles (CFR: 1926)
1961-65 John A. McCone (CFR: 1958)
1965-66 Vice Adm. William F. Raborn, Jr.
1966-73 Richard Helms (CFR: Date Unk)
1973   James R. Schlesinger (CFR: 1986)
1973-76 William E. Colby (CFR: 1975)
1976-77 George H.W. Bush (CFR: 1971)
1977-81 Adm. Stansfield Turner (CFR: 1973)
1981-87 William J. Casey (CFR: 1973)
1987-90 William H. Webster (CFR: 1987)
1990-93 Robert Gates (CFR: 1983)
1993-   James Woolsey (CFR 1975)

Chairmen, Senate Select Committee on Intelligence

1976-77   Daniel K. Inouye, (D. Hawaii)
1977-81   Birch Bayh, (D. Indiana, CFR: 1971)
1981-85   Barry Goldwater, (R. Arizona)
1985-87   David Durenberger, (R. Minnesota)
1987-   David Boren, (D. Oklahoma, CFR: 1989)

Chairmen, House Permanent Select Committee on Intelligence

1977-85   Edward P. Boland, (D. Massachusetts)
1985-87   Lee H. Hamilton, (D. Indiana)
1987-89   Louis Stokes, (D. Ohio CFR: 1988))
1989-   Anthony C. Beilenson, (D. California)

President Bill Clinton's CFR Cabinet Appointments

Secretary of Defense: Les Aspin (CFR 1973)

Secretary of Health and Human Services: Donna E. Shalala (CFR 1982)

Secretary of Housing and Urban Development: Henry G. Cisneros (CFR 1982)

Secretary of Interior: Bruce Babbit (CFR 1980)

Secretary of State: Warren M. Christopher (CFR 1973)

Secretary of the Treasury: Lloyd Bentsen (CFR 1973)

Presidential Affiliation With CFR (since 1921)

Herbert Hoover (CFR: 1937) (Stock Market crash of 1929—government begins borrowing money through Federal Reserve; beginning of current national debt)

Franklin Roosevelt (CFR: 1928) (New Deal programs and World War II increases National Debt)

Harry S. Truman (Administration staffed by CFR members) (Cold War begins; Arms race begins—National Debt increases)

Dwight D. Eisenhower (CFR: 1949) (Cold War and Arms Race continues, Space Race begins—National Debt increases)

John F. Kennedy (refused membership, but Administration staffed by over 60 CFR members) (Cold War continues; Arms Race continues; National Debt increases)

Lyndon B. Johnson (Inherited Kennedy's staff of CFR members)(War in Vietnam begins and escalates, massive social welfare programs instituted—National Debt increases)

Richard M. Nixon (CFR: 1961) (War in Vietnam continues, phases out, Arms Race continues, Social Welfare programs increased—National Debt increases)

Gerald Ford (Administration staffed by CFR members) (Cold War continues, Social Welfare programs increase—National Debt increases)

James E. Carter (CFR: 1983) (Cold War continues, Iran deposes Shaw, Panama Canal given away, Social Welfare programs continue and grow—National Debt increases)

APPENDIX

Ronald Reagan (Administration staffed by over 80 CFR members)(Cold War continues, Social Welfare peaks out temporarily—National Debt increases)

George Bush (CFR: 1971) (Cold War ends, Desert Shield/Storm takes place, Social Welfare programs grow, Foreign Aid increases drastically)

Bill Clinton (CFR: 1990) (Social Welfare programs increase drastically, Taxes soar to highest rates ever, interest rates plunge, Government spending increases, demanding more government borrowing—National Debt to international investment bankers grows to all-time high, U.S. troop commitments to United Nations sets new precedents in military reinforcement of global affairs)

Secretaries of State
who were CFR members:

Robert Lansing
Charles Evans Hughes
Frank B. Kellogg
Henry L. Stimson
Cordell Hull
Edward R. Stettinius
George Marshall
Dean Acheson
John Foster Dulles
Christian Herter
Dean Rusk
William F. Rogers
Henry Kissinger
Cyrus Vance
Edmund Muskie
Alexander Haig
George Shultz
James Baker
Warren M. Christopher

Secretaries of War/Defense
who were CFR members:

Newton N. Barker
Dwight F. Davis
Henry L. Stimson
Robert Paterson
James Forrestal
George Marshall
Robert Lovett
Charles Wilson
Neal H. McElroy
Thomas S. Gates, Jr.
Robert S. McNamara
Elliott Richardson
James Schlesinger
Donald Rumsfield
Harold Brown
Caspar Weinberger
Frank Carlucci
Richard Cheney
Les Aspin

Endnotes

1. For additional information concerning the autopsy and the medical evidence, see *Best Evidence* by David Lifton.

2. Three Boeing 707s were purchased by the Air Force during the Eisenhower administration, but they were designated as Military Airlift Command aircraft. Though Eisenhower utilized these airplanes, they were not used for the sole purpose of transporting the president. All three of these aircraft were C-137A models. The difference between the A and the B designation was the type of engine. The "A" had the standard early design turbojets and the "B" had the fan-jets. The tail number of these aircraft were 86970, 86971, and 86972. 86970, after re-engining to the "B" configuration, became the presidential backup aircraft and was the airplane that transported Lyndon Johnson to Dallas.

3. It is interesting to note that in this time frame George Bush was the chairman of the board of Zapata Offshore Company of Houston. He was also the co-founder and director of Zapata petroleum corporation. Coincidentally, two ships used in Operation ZAPATA were re-named *Houston* and *Barbara* for the event. After Kennedy's death, a "George Bush of the CIA" was briefed on the FBI investigation of the assassination, according to an FBI memo written to Hoover. Though denying to an investigative journalist that he was *that* George Bush, in 1976, he became director of the CIA—quite an accomplishment for someone without an intelligence background within the "Company."

4. All motivational aspects of assassination, including the Bay of Pigs debacle, can be found in *Crossfire; The Plot That Killed Kennedy*, by Jim Marrs.

5. Further information concerning the Hoover connection to the Kennedy Assassination, particularly in dealing with the post-murder coverup, can be found in *Act of Treason* by Mark North.

6. Southeast Asia had been divided between the Pentagon and the CIA. The military operational area was South Vietnam, while the CIA and certain Special Forces units under their operational control conducted a covert war in Laos. This Laotian operation, conducted out of Vientiane, was known as Operation WHITESTAR. The funds to run the operation came from profits derived from the sale of opium, which was locally grown and distributed abroad.

7. Early versions of the AR-15 had been purchased by the Air Force to arm security police as early as 1964, but after 1967, all M-16s were built by Colt.

8. For more information on Operation PAPERCLIP and the secret removal of Nazi war criminals from Europe by the U.S. Government, see: *The Paperclip Conspiracy* by Tom Bower; *Secret Agenda* by Linda Hunt; and *The Belarus Secret* by John Loftus.

For more on John J. McCloy and his involvement in the Joint War-Navy Coordinating Committee (JWNCC) in World War II, the California Japanese-American segregation camps, the Nuremburg trials, the OSS, the World Bank for Reconstruction, the Chase-Manhattan Bank, the Council of Foreign Affairs, Lyndon Johnson's staff, Kennedy's staff, and the Rockefeller's Standard Oil, see *The Chairman* by Kai Bird.

9. Lady Bird Johnson held title in name only. This permitted Johnson to claim that he did not have a conflict of interest because the huge profits made from his illicit dealings were going to his wife, not to him personally. (*The Texas Connection*, by Craig I. Zirbel, pgs 116-117).

10. Brown and Root also was awarded the $90 million dollar contract on a "cost plus" basis to build the NASA Space Center 22 miles from Houston on a desolate tract of land owned by a Texas oil company. The oil company, as was Brown and Root, happened to be one of Johnson's supporters. The oil company retained all surrounding land, which quickly increased in value as the NASA facility was developed. At the time the decisions were made, Johnson was the head of the Space Council.

11. I selected the ending year of 1968 for several reasons. It was the year of the greatest rate of attrition of equipment due to the TET-68 Lunar New Year battles, and it was two years into the adaption of the M-16.

12. At a meeting in September, 1962, between Carlos Marcello (real name: Calogero Minacore) and Edward Becker, a Las Vegas gambler, Marcello stated (as recorded by the FBI's ELSUR electronic surveillance program) "Don't worry about that little Bobby son-of-a-bitch. He's going to be taken care of. *Livarsi na petra di la scarpa.*" (Take the stone out of my shoe). From another meeting, the statement was made: "You don't kill a dog by cutting off his tail. You kill him by cutting off his head." This was in regard to getting rid of Bobby Kennedy by getting rid of his brother. A new president would appoint a new attorney general.

13. This would put the stateroom, a small bedroom, the farthest possible distance from where Kennedy's coffin was carried at the rear of the plane.

14. Military staffs at Battalion, Regimental and Brigade level are numbered. At this level the designator is "S." At Division level it is "G." The S-3, or operations officer, at Brigade level would have a G-3 counterpart at Division or Corps.

15. Some researchers have identified the "Umbrella Man" in Dealey Plaza as giving a signal by opening and closing his umbrella as the motorcade appeared. Another man, wearing a walkie-talkie on his belt, was noticed near the corner of Main and Houston. Most witnesses assumed he was a Secret Service agent, as he transmitted on his radio as the motorcade turned the corner. The Secret Service denies an agent was there.

16. Reported in a televised interview with Neal Sheehan of the Washington-based Christic Institute.

17. The Ranch differentiates this place in normal conversation between CIA operatives from "the Farm," which is the paramilitary training center in Virginia on the grounds of Camp Perry.

18. When LBJ was finally briefed on the activities of ZR/RIFLE in Central and South American countries, he exclaimed, "My God! We're running a damned Murder Incorporated down there."

19. Sometime during the planning phase Marcello voiced his idea of using a dupe. According to Edward Becker, a Las Vegas private investigator, Marcello wanted to used a "nut" for the job who could be manipulated so that the killing could not be traced back to Marcello.

20. The reasons the Corsicans were chosen were simple. The Mafia needed white men; They could not go to Beirut or Hong Kong, the two other principle centers for hiring assassins at the time; They needed skilled and experienced assassins who would do the job the first time without botching it, then be able to disappear; They had to be untraceable locally (inside the U.S.); They needed skilled killers, who, if caught, could not be linked to the American Mafia, and who were not known to the American police; And finally, they needed people who would not talk if caught—people who lived by the "code of silence."

21. Lucien Sarti, who was reported to be the Mafia supplied shooter of the two-man rifle team on the Grassy Knoll, was killed in Mexico City in 1972.

22. The two brothers referred to are probably Ignacio and Guillermo *Novo*, members of Operation 40—and possibley ZR/RIFLE—who in 1964 fired a bazooka against the United Nations building. In 1976, Guillermo was convicted of being an accessory to the assassination of former chilean ambassador Orlando Letelier in Washington, D.C.

23. A more complete form of this transcript can be found in Mark Lane's *Plausible Denial (pgs 295-303)*, Thunder Mouth's Press, NY.

24. It is a continuing issue of debate whether or not the "Umbrella Man," who was standing near the freeway sign, was the one who initiated the ambush by opening and closing his umbrella. This author believes that the visual signal was used as a backup "all-clear to open fire" or "the mission-is-a-go" sign to any of the kill teams whose walkie-talkie radios might have malfunctioned. The Umbrella Man's partner appears in some photographs to have a small box or radio on his belt on sticking out of his back pocket.

25. Some researchers claim that the "Umbrella Man" sitting on the curb on the north side of Elm actually held a super-secret CIA assassination weapon that fired poisoned darts. It is true that the KGB had an assassination umbrella that fired a tiny steel pellet containing poison with compressed air, but it had no range. It was a contact weapon. The OSS, however, did utilize various flechette type darts in weapons in World War II and it is possible such a weapon existed in 1963.

26. It has been reported that Lyndon Johnson, riding in a black Cadillac with Senator Ralph Yarborough two cars behind Kennedy's Lincoln, dove to the floorboard as his car turned the 120 degree corner—*before the first shot rang out!*

27. *Crossfire*, pgs 315-316.

28. One part of basic training is known as the "infiltration course." It consists of crawling around, under and beside various obstacles toward an objective. As the trainees are negotiating the course, machineguns fire just over their heads in traversing fire to lend realism to the exercise.

29. In those days the Dallas Police Department, as were most departments, demanded that all uniform officers wear their hats at any time they were out of a vehicle or building. To be caught without a uniform hat meant disciplinary action. However, attempting to shoot a rifle mounted with a telescopic sight would be almost impossible while wearing a typical steeply-billed police uniform hat.

30. Lucien Sarti and Roscoe White.

31. From videotape interview conducted by Mark Lane. Additional description of this incident can be found in *On The Trail Of The Assassins* by Jim Garrison, New Orleans District Attorney at the time of the assassination.

32. The Carcano was somehow determined by the FBI within hours of the shooting to have been purchased by Lee Harvey Oswald, using an alias of A.J. Hidell, through Klein's Sporting Goods, a Chicago mail order gun dealer. It has never been explained exactly how this was done. Even if the rifle was traced through Federal customs records, the tracing would have taken days at best.

33. In 1978, the recording was analyzed by computer enhancement by acoustics expert Dr. James Barger. The 5.5 minutes of "stuck microphone" radio recording was filtered until a computer graph of sound impulses 500 feet long was produced. According to the results, at least four shots were fired. Three from the rear, and one from the Grassy Knoll.

34. Statement made in a deposition by Marita Lorenz. *Plausible Denial*, by Mark Lane, pg 303.

35. Osborne's identity is presented in *Called To Serve*, by LtCol. James Gritz, USA (Ret).

36. 90 days after Oswald defected to Russia, an obsolete SAM-2 missile shot CIA U-2 pilot Francis Gary Powers out of the sky over Russian territory. This incident effectively cancelled the arms summit between Eisenhower and Kruschev scheduled to occur in Switzerland. In the past, the SAM-2 could not knock down the U-2s because the Russians did not know what altitude the Lockheed spyplanes flew at.

37. Texas Attorney General Waggoner Carr's and Dallas District Attorney Henry Wade's (both former FBI agents) assertion that Oswald was a paid informant for the FBI was presented to the Warren

Commission. It was given in secret to Rankin and Warren on 1/24/64. But the Commission chose to believe J. Edgar Hoover when he told them that Oswald had never worked in any capacity for the FBI.

38. Oswald was interrogated for 12 hours on Friday, the 22nd of November; 3 hours on Saturday the 23rd, and 1 hour on Sunday the 24th.

39. *Best Evidence*, pgs 681-683, 701-702. The helicopter flight to Walter Reed took about 6 minutes, leaving 30 minutes for the procedure to be accomplished and the body transferred to Bethesda.

40. *Best Evidence*, pgs 683, 701-702.

41. *Historical Highlights of Andrews Air Force Base; 1942-1989*, pg 233.

42. *Best Evidence*, pgs 600-603.

43. *JFK: Conspiracy of Silence*, pgs 84-85.

44. Twin Cities was one of the arsenals that built military ammunition for the military.

45. See *The Chairman; John J. McCloy and the Making of the American Establishment* by Kai Bird, Simon & Schuster, NY, 1993.

46. Mark Lane: "Sixty-eight percent of the people in Dealy Plaza, told by the FBI to commit perjury, who saw something they will never forget—the death of their President in front of their eyes—went forward and told the truth."

47. Marina Oswald had an uncle who was a colonel in the KGB. She knew how easy it would be for the FBI to make arrangements with the Immigration and Naturalization Service to evict her from the country. It was common in Russia for anyone running afoul of the intelligence services or Communist party organs to be exiled to Siberia.

48. *Called to Serve*, pg 537.

49. *Best Evidence*, pgs 370-371.

50. *Called To Serve*, pg 561.

51. The debunkers point out that the term "Navy Int." is incorrect and such messages would have bore the identifier "ONI" for Office of Naval Intelligence. This would be the case—unless the sender used a false moniker for purposes of disavowment at a later date if discovered. According to LTC Gritz, such a "discriminator" is often used as a code to positively authenticate sensitive instructions contained on the message.

52. *On The Trail Of The Assassins*, pg 42.

53. Researcher Ralph Shoenman relates that "E. Howard Hunt set up a dummy organization called the 'Cuban Revolutionary Council.' The Headquarters was none other than 544 Camp Street in New Orleans...Bannister was connected with the FBI, David Ferrie to the CIA, and Oswald to the ONI—and carried contract number S-172 with the FBI—and all were sharing offices with Howard Hunt of the CIA. All of these were connected to Clay Shaw, an "international businessman" and former OSS officer."

54. On August 18th, 1992, the author respond to this jaded article with a 15 page response that dismantled each and every pro-Warren Commission assertion. The response to this detailed letter from the editorial staff of the magazine was brief and non-committal: "Thank you for your letter about our cover story, "JFK — The Untold Story of the Warren Commission." Your comments have been read with interest and shared with the appropriate editors. It was thoughtful of you to write." It was signed, "Michael Ruby," the magazine's editor.

55. LBJ's mistress, who was interviewed for a television documentary, stated that Johnson told her that when the files are finally opened, "there won't be anything there."

56. *By Way Of Deception*, by Victor Ostrovsky, pgs 141-143.

57. *Orange County Register*—World Briefly, July 21, 1992.

58. See Appendix for a copy of NSM 273, which was discovered quite by accident in the archives of the LBJ Library. Of particular note is the passage of the memo that stated it must be "plausibly deniable" should it be discovered.

59. Prouty, pg 97.

60. Prouty, pg 116.

61. *Passing the Torch*, pg 199, "The Vietnam Experience" series, Boston Publishing Co. Boston, MA.

62. Rees, Elfan ap, *World Military Helicopters*, pgs 35-37, Jane's Publishing Company, London, 1986.

63. Prouty, pg 109.

64. Bell/Textron production during Vietnam:

Model	Total
UH-1A	173
UH-1B	1010
UH-1C	749
UH-1D	2008*
UH-1F	120
OH-58	2200
AH-1G	1127

*The D model was phased out in 1967 in favor of the more powerful UH-1H, but total numbers available to the author include those produced "to present" and therefore did not reflect those produced only during Vietnam. Also, it should be noted that three other variants were built (HH-1H, EH-1H and UH-1V) but were in small quantities and not reported by number.

65. OPLAN 34A was broken down to three phases. Phase One consisted of USAF U-2 flights across the skies of North Vietnam and commando raids conducted by South Vietnamese marines and Nationalist Chinese mercenaries. Phase Two called for 25-40 bombers, marked as Royal Laotian aircraft and flown by U.S. and Thai pilots, to take off from Laos and strike targets in North Vietnam. Phase three would send American destroyers into the Gulf of Tonkin to prod the North Vietnamese into visibly "forcing" Johnson's hand.

66. Prouty, pg 324.

67. *The Vietnam War*, pg 74, Crown publishers, NYC, 1983.

68. *It's A Conspiracy*, pg 110.

69. Operation Starlite was originally designated Operation Satellite, however a clerk made an error in typing the operational plan and when it went out to the field regiments, it became Operation Starlite. The operation, a search and destroy mission, occurred during 18-19 August 1965 in the area surrounding the Van Tuong village complexes and Phuoc Than Peninsula 9 miles south of Chu Lai. The operation, which was virtually kept secret from the South Vietnamese command staff until the last minute, was a complete success. Under Krulak's support, the Marines landed in four places around the coastal area (three heli-team LZs and one amphibious assault) and successfully caught 1,500 hardcore Vietcong main force guerrillas of the 1st VC Regiment, 52nd VC Company and 45th Weapons Battalion completely by surprise. After sweeping eastward to the coast, the Marines pressed the Vietcong against the sea and engaged them in a last-stand effort on the communists' part. The end result was 614 VC killed by honest body count, 9 prisoners taken, and 49 suspects detained. Cost to the Marines was 45 KIA and 203 WIA. (Shulimson, Jack, and Johnson, Charles M. *U.S Marines in Vietnam, The Landing And The Buildup, 1965*, pgs 69-81) U.S. Marine Corps, Washington DC, 1978.

70. Lyndon Johnson, when he was a Senator during World War II, activated his naval reserve commission and volunteered to go on a fact finding mission to the South Pacific. When he arrived, no less than General MacArthur met him and made arrangements for him to fly as an observer on a bombing mission. During the flight the airplane he rode in as a passenger was attacked by a Japanese Zero. After a brief firing pass, the Zero left and the bomber returned to base. MacArthur was waiting, and when Johnson crawled out of the plane, the general awarded him the Silver Star for bravery. No one else in the crew received an award. Johnson returned to Washington a war hero. There has always been a question if the "Zero" that made the "firing pass" on the bomber was actually a solo Japanese plane or a convenient stand-in.

McNamara served during World War II as a logistical strategist for Bomber Command. John J. McCloy served as an artillery operations officer during World War I, but saw little action from his "in-the-rear" protected position.

71. Krulak, Victor, *First To Fight*, pg 221, Pocket Books, NYC 1991.

72. Krulak, Victor H., Lt. Gen. USMC (Ret), *First To Fight*, pg 222, Pocket Books, NY, 1991.

73. Ibid, pg 224.

74. Krulak, pg 226.

75. Incredibly, the U.S. forces in Vietnam were shackled by Secretary of Defense McNamara's Rules of Engagement (ROE). The ROE consisted of such ridiculous rules as:

1. U.S. troops could not fire at Vietcong unless first fired upon.

2. Vehicles more than 200 yards off the Ho Chi Minh Trail could not be attacked.

3. NVAF MiGs could not be attacked unless they were airborne and posed a threat. MiG fighters on a runway could not be struck.

4. Surface-to-air (SAM) missile sites could not be attacked while they were under construction. They could only be attacked after they became operational.

5. Vietcong and NVA units could not be pursued if they crossed over the border into Cambodia or Laos.

6. Hanoi and Haiphong could not be bombed. This permitted many SAM batteries to be taken out of the cities and concentrated in other areas, increasing the danger to U.S. aircraft.

76. It should be noted here that the contract to dredge Camh Ranh Bay was worth hundreds of millions of dollars of taxpayers money. When Lyndon Johnson died, he left over $20,000.000 to his estate. It has been estimated that even if he saved every honest dollar he made as a politician and in other legal investments, he would have been lucky to have earned 1/10 as much.

77. *The Vietnam Experience*, pg 68, Boston Publishing Company.

78. *War in the Shadows*, pg 71, The Vietnam Experience, Boston Publishing Co.

79. *CIA, The Secret Files*, Part 2, "Phoenix Rising."

80. Ibid.

81. Ibid.

82. It should be noted that the failures in combat operations in Korea resulted because of the United Nations command structure. All major operations and all air ops had to be cleared through United Nations headquarters in New York through and office in the U.N. that is held *by a Soviet General!* As soon as the Soviets knew of the operational plans, the Chinese and North Koreans knew. This office has always been held by a Soviet General.

83. The ZR/RIFLE assassination team, headed by E. Howard Hunt, included: Rafael "Chi Chi" Quintero, Raul Villaverde, Luis Posada Carilles (AKA Ramon Medina), Felix Rodriquez, Frank Fiorini (Sturgis), Ricardo Chavez, and Joaquin Sanjenis. This is approximanty half of the original membership. (*Shadow Government*, pgs 4-8).

84. *Shadow Government*, pgs 4-8, 206-214.

85. All of these men had formerly worked for Operation 40, the ZR/RIFLE infiltration, sabotage and assassination team, out of the JM/WAVE Miami CIA station. The JM/WAVE station chief was Theodore Shackley, whose second in command was Thomas Clines. Both were to move on to Laos to run the CIA operation there, which depended upon drug money for operational capital.

86. The Plumbers had been quite active. In 1969, they appeared at Chappaquiddick to look for dirt on Edward Kennedy, then in 1971, they broke into the office of Daniel Ellsberg's psychiatrist. Ellsberg had been determined to be the leak behind the "Pentagon Papers."

87. E. Howard Hunt has lately come forward and added one further motivation for the break-in. He stated during a television documentary on the 20th anniversary of Watergate that the burglars were also instructed to photograph the financial records of the DNC. This was to provide to the White House any evidence gained of foreign contributions to the Democratic campaign fund which might be used against the Democrats.

88. Nixon, who served as a supply officer in the Pacific, returned to his home state of California and entered law practice in Whittier, a suburb of Los Angeles.

89. Ambrose, Stephen E., *Eisenhower*, Vol. 1, pg 437, Simon & Schuster, New York, 1983.

90. *Human Events*, December 2, 1959.

91. A "New World Order" was the catch phrase for Rockefeller's campaign. It had also been a often heard phrase at the UN convention in San Francisco in 1947, and continued through the years to rise again during the Bush years—especially when the Berlin Wall was demolished and the Soviet Union broke up. Bush, in his flowery speech describing the event, stated that "...there is now a New World Order...."

92. *U.S. News & World Report* in 1971 stated that: "It was on the advice of Governor Rockefeller, who described Mr. Kissinger as 'the smartest guy available,' that Mr. Nixon chose him for his top adviser on foreign policy."

93. Most major newspapers and two television networks are owned by members of the CFR.

94. *Washington Star*, January 21, 1970.

95. *New York Times*, January 31, 1971.

96. In January, 1964, newsmen asked Nelson Rockefeller when he had first thought about being president of the United States. He replied: "Ever since I was a kid. After all, when you think of what I had, what else was there to aspire to?"

97. John Dean told the investigating committee chaired by Sam Ervin that Nixon had known of the coverup being perpetrated by his staff. A month later, former White House aide Alexander Butterfield revealed that Nixon, as a matter of routine, had covertly recorded conversations in his offices. Both Archibald Cox and Ervin pressed the White House for the tapes, but Nixon, citing Executive Privilege, refused to relinquish them. He then tried to fire Cox, but Attorney General Elliot L. Richardson refused to follow through, resigning in protest instead. His deputy, William Ruckelshaus, also refused and was fired. Nixon's solicitor general, who was next in the chain of command, then fired Cox. These events became known as the "Saturday Night Massacre" and led to heightened suspicions that Nixon definitely had something to hide.

98. *Current Biography—1947*, pg 409.

99. Bird, Kai, *The Chairman; John J. McCloy, the Making of the American Establishment*, pg 628. Simon & Schuster, NY, 1993.

100. Ibid.

101. McCloy was also one of the "Wise Men" who advised Lyndon Johnson during the Vietnam war. As such, the group of advisors pressed Johnson to continue to send more troops, drop more bombs on worthless targets, spend more money on war material and fight against popular opinion, until one day in 1967 when they simply told Johnson that it was all a big mistake, and he would have to explain it to the American people. They simply shrugged their shoulders and walked out of the Oval Office. One week later Johnson made his famous "I will not run again" speech.

102. Epperson, A. Ralph, *The Unseen Hand*, pg 140, Publius Press, Tucson, AZ, 1985.

103. Mullins, Eustace. *Secrets of the Federal Reserve; the London Connection*, pgs 55-56, Bankers Research Institute, Staunton, VA, 1984.

104. *The Unseen Hand*, pg 140.

105. Ibid, pg 131.

106. Ibid.

107. Ibid, pg 133.

108. Salmon Porter Chase, former radical Republican governor of Ohio, was a prima donna in Lincoln's cabinet. As Secretary of the Treasury, Chase was constantly at odds with other members—especially William H. Seward, Lincoln's Secretary of State, who in 1861, suggested a diversionary foreign war to reunite the country. Chase's

constant backstairs political dealings with certain senators and bankers finally caught up with him in 1864 and he was ousted from the cabinet. Lincoln, always one to forgive and forget, promptly appointed him Chief Justice of the Supreme Court.

109. Kennan, H.S., *The Federal Reserve Bank*, pg 9.

110. Owen, Robert L., *National Economy and the Banking System*, pgs 99-100.

111. "Booth" was located hiding in a barn near Port Royal, Virginia, three days after escaping from Washington. He was shot by a soldier named Boston Corbett, who fired without orders. Whether or not the man that was killed was Booth is still a matter of contention, but the fact remains that whoever it was that was killed had no chance to identify himself. Incredibly, it was Secretary of War Edwin Stanton who made the final identification.

112. Jacob Schiff would later invest $20 million in the Bolshevik Revolution (1917).

113. J.P. Morgan Sr. made a small fortune in one deal with the Federal government when he purchased 5,000 defective carbines that had been declared dangerous and obsolete, and sold them back to the U.S. Army at a massive profit. In 1861, shortly after the war began, Morgan found out about a new Union regiment being formed in St. Louis that required weapons. At about the same time, he learned of the large surplus offering of carbines being surplused at an armory in New York at $3.50 each. He telegraphed the Union commander and offered the carbines as "new carbines in perfect condition" for $22.00 each. The commander agreed to the price, and Morgan went to the bank to borrow the money for the initial purchase using the contract as collateral. He then wired the armory the funds and ordered the weapons sent to St. Louis. He never even saw them. Nor did he invest a single penny of his own. But when the regiment began experiencing troubles with the carbines, such as having them blow up when being fired, and attempted to sue Morgan, the court inexplicably

ruled in Morgan's favor and instructed the government to pay Morgan in full the sum of $109,912. The government had purchased its own useless property at great profit to Morgan. (*It's A Conspiracy* pgs 163-164).

114. Vanderlip, Frank, "Farm Boy to Financier," *Saturday Evening Post*, Feb. 8, 1935.

115. Involved behind the scenes of the elections of both Woodrow Wilson and Franklin Roosevelt, and their subsequent policy making, was "Colonel" Edward Mandell House (who never served in the military). House, son of Civil War Rothschild agent Thomas W. House, was a charter member of the Council on Foreign Relations and represented the interests of the major New York City bankers and the Rothschilds. House was originally a member of the Institute of International Affairs, formed in Paris at the Majestic Hotel in a secret meeting on May 30, 1919. Its American branch, formed on July 29, 1921, became the Council on Foreign Relations.

116. Allen, Gary, "The Bankers, Conspiratorial Origins of the Federal Reserve," *American Opinion*, March, 1978, pg 16.

117. Bell, Don, "Who Are Our Rulers?," *American Mercury*, September 1960, pg 136.

118. Courtney, Phoebe and Kent, *America's Unelected Rulers: The Council on Foreign Relations*, Conservative Society of America, New Orleans, 1962, pgs 1-2.

119. Roosevelt, Edith Kermit, "Elite Clique Holds Power in U.S.," *Indianapolis News*, Dec. 23, 1961.

120. Cecil Rhodes, diamond magnate and founder of Rhodesia, was a globalist who felt that the world should be ruled by one government. He founded the Rhodes scholarship program to further this idea through continuing to educate the future generations of the elite. Rhodes, like Alexander Hamilton before him, felt that there were two classes of

people: the aristocrats and the masses. The aristocrats were destined to govern and obtain wealth at the expense of the masses.

121. Hefler, James C. *Are Textbooks Harming Your Children?*, Mott Media, Milford, MI. Pg 30.

122. Allen, Gary, "New Education," *American Opinion.*

123. *The Unseen Hand*, pg 386.

124. John Dewey helped found the American branch of the socialist British Fabian Society in 1905. In 1921, the Society changed its name to the League for Industrial Democracy, and announced its purpose as "education for a new social order based on production for use and not for profit." Dewey later became this organization's president. Later, he went to Russia to help organize a Marxist educational system, but even Stalin could not tolerate the liberal and forced him to leave the country. His Russian students were banished to Siberia. (*Unseen Hand* pgs 386-387).

125. "Occasional Letter, No. 1," General Education Board, 1904.

126. "N.E.A., Education for a Global Community," *Freeman Digest*, pg 1.

127. The globalists find Christianity a major roadblock to their agenda. Of all the world's religions, Christianity is the only one that reads the New Testament. And it is in the New Testament where one finds the prophecies of the Book of Revelation that warns of many of the future plans of the globalists. For this reason, almost a fourth of the world's population may resist changes that lead to a global government, currency, army and religion.

128. Of the $5 dollar denomination, the U.S. Treasury printed 63,360,000 ($316,800,000).

Bibliography

Books

Asprey, Robert B. *War in the Shadows*, New York: Doubleday, 1975.

Bamford, James, *The Puzzle Palace; A Report on America's Most Secret Agency*, New York: Penguin Books, 1985.

Bank, Colonel Aaron, USA (Ret), *From Oss to Green Berets*, San Francisco: Presidio Press, 1986.

Barron, John, *KGB Today; The Hidden Hand*, New York: Reader's Digest Press, 1983.

Barron, John, *KGB; The Secret Work of Soviet Agents*, New York: Bantam, 1974.

Bird, Kai, *The Chairman; John J. McCloy—The Making of the American Establishment*, New York: Simon & Schuster, 1992.

Bower, Tom, *The Paperclip Conspiracy; The Hunt for the Nazi Scientists*, Boston: Little, Brown and Company, 1987.

Brown, Anthony Cave, *Bodyguard of Lies*, New York: Harper & Row, 1975.

Cantelon, Willard, *The Day The Dollar Dies*, Plainfield, NJ,: 1973.

Crenshaw, Charles A., with Hansen, Jens and Shaw, J. Gary, *JFK; Conspiracy of Silence*, New York: Signet, 1992.

Davis, John H., *The Kennedys, Dynasty and Disaster*, New York: SPI books, 1992.

Dobson, Christopher, and Payne, Ronald, *The Terrorists; Their Weapons, Leaders and Tactics*, New York: Facts On File, 1979.

Donigan, Robert L., and Fisher, Edward C., *The Evidence Handbook*, Evanston, Ill.: The Traffic Institute, 1972.

Dubby, James P., and Ricci, Vincent L., *The Assassination of John F. Kennedy; A Complete Book of Facts*, New York: Thunder's Mouth Press, 1992.

Dunnigan, James F. and Nofi, Albert A., *Dirty Little Secrets; Military Information You're Not Supposed to Know*, New York: William Morrow, 1990.

Epperson, A. Ralph, *The Unseen Hand*, Tucson, AZ,: Pablius Press, 1985.

Garrison, Jim, *On the Trail of the Assassins*, New York: Warner, 1988.

Gritz, Col. James "Bo", *Called to Serve*, Sandy Valley, NV,: Lazarus Publishing, 1991.

Groden, Robert J., and Livingstone, Harrision Edward, *High Treason; The Assassination of President John F. Kennedy and the New Evidence of Conspiracy*, New York: Berkley Books, 1989.

Hunt, Linda, *Secret Agenda; The United States Government, Nazi Scientists, and Project Paperclip, 1945 to 1990*, New York: St. Martin's Press, 1991.

Johnson, Loch K., *America's Secret Power; The CIA in a Democratic Society*, New York: Oxford University Press, 1989.

Lane, Mark, *Plausible Denial: Was the CIA Involved in the Assassination of JFK?*, New York: Thunder's Mouth Press, 1991.

Lewis, David A., and Hicks, Darryl E., *The Presidential Zero-Year Mystery*, Plainfield, NJ,: Logos International, 1980.

236

BIBLIOGRAPHY

Lifton, David S., *Best Evidence*, New York: Carroll & Graf, 1988.

Marchetti, Victor, and Marks, John D., *The CIA and the Cult of Intelligence*, New York: Dell, 1980.

Marks, John, *The Search for the Manchurian Candidate*, New York: W.W. Norton & Co., 1979.

Marrs, Jim, *Crossfire; The Plot That Killed Kennedy*, New York: Carroll & Graf, 1989.

Marshall, Jonathan, and Scott, Peter Dale and Hunter, Jane, *The Iran-Contra Connection; Secret Teams and Covert Operations in the Reagan Era*, Boston: South End Press, 1987.

McDonald, Hugh, *Appointment in Dallas*, New York: the Hugh McDonald Publishing Corp., 1992.

Menninger, Bonar, *Mortal Error; The Shot That Killed JFK*, New York: St. Martin's Press, 1992.

Morin, Relman, *Dwight D. Eisenhower; A Gauge of Greatness*, New York: Simon & Schuster, 1969.

Mullins, Eustace, *Secrets of the Federal Reserve*, Staunton, VA,: Bankers Research Institute, 1984.

North, Mark, *Act of Treason*, New York: Carroll & Graf, 1991.

Ostrovsky, Victor, and Hoy, Claire, *By Way of Deception*, New York: St. Martin's Press. 1990.

O'Toole, G.J.A., *Honorable Treachery; A History of U.S. Intelligence, Espionage, and Covert Action from the American Revolution to the CIA*, New York: Atlantic Monthly Press, 1991.

Perloff, James, *The Shadows of Power; The Council on Foreign Relations and the American Decline*, Boston: Western Islands Publishers, 1988.

Prouty, L. Fletcher, *JFK: The CIA, Vietnam, and the plot to assassinate John F. Kennedy*, New York: Birch Lane Press, 1992.

Robbins, Christopher, *Air America*, New York: Avon, 1990.

Robbins, Christopher, *The Ravens*, New York: Pocket Books, 1989.

Robertson, Pat, *The New World Order*, Dallas: New Word Publishing, 1991.

Russell, Dick, *The Man Who Knew Too Much*, New York: Carroll & Graf, 1992.

Shaw, L. Gary, and Harris, Larry, *Coverup*, Dallas, TX,: 1976.

Simpson, Charles M. III, *Inside the Green Berets; The First Thirty Years*, San Francisco: Presidio Press, 1983.

Still, William T., *New World Order; The Ancient Plan of Secret Societies*, Lafayette, LA.,: Huntington House Publishers, 1990.

Vankin, Jonathan, *Conspiracies, Cover-ups, and Crimes; Political Manipulation and Mind Control in America*, New York: Paragon House, 1992.

Volkman, Ernest, and Baggett, Blaine, *Secret Intelligence*, New York: Doubleday, 1989.

Weberman, Alan J., and Canfield, Michael, *Coup D'Etat In America*, San Francisco: Quick American Archives, 1992.

BIBLIOGRAPHY

Welsh, Douglas, *The History of the Vietnam War*, New York: Galahad Books, 1981.

Woodward, Bob, *Veil; The Secret Wars of the CIA, 1981-1987*, New York: Pocket Books, 1988.

Zirbel, Craig I., *The Texas Connection; The Assassination of John F. Kennedy*, Scottsdale, AZ,: The Texas Connection Co., 1991.

Miss. Publications

The Vietnam War, New York: Crown Publishers, 1983.

Historical Highlights of Andrews Air Force Base 1942-1989, Office of History, 177th Air Base Wing, Andrews Air Force Base.

Hearing Before The Subcommittee On Oversight and Investigation of the Committee On Veterans' Affairs, House of Representatives, Washington D.C., 1982.

The Warren Commission Report, Washington D.C.,: President's Commission of the Assassination of President Kennedy, September 24, 1964.

Inside the Shadow Government, Delcaration of Plaintiffs' Counsel filed by the Christic Institute, U.S. District Court, Miami FL., March 31, 1988.

The Vietnam Experince: War in the Shadows, Boston: Boston Publishing Co., 1988.

Janes Encyclopedia of Aviation, compiled by Michael J.H. Taylor, New York: Portland House, 1980.

American Military History, Department of the Army, 1953.

INDEX

INDEX

241

KILL ZONE

INDEX

INDEX

INDEX

INDEX

247

INDEX

INDEX

KILL ZONE